ISBN 978-1-330-62779-2
PIBN 10084443

THE CRISIS
IN CHURCH and COLLEGE

BY

G. W. McPHERSON

VOLUME I.

THIS BOOK IS DEDICATED TO THE DEITY OF OUR LORD
JESUS CHRIST AND THE INSPIRATION
OF THE BIBLE

SOLD BY THE AUTHOR AT

34 SAINT ANDREW'S PLACE,
YONKERS, N. Y.

Copyright, 1919, by
G. W. McPHERSON

PREFACE

THE manuscript for this volume was read by Rev. W. M. Griffith Thomas, D.D., of Wycliffe College, Toronto, and the revision was carefully made on the basis of his valuable suggestions. The author is indebted to this distinguished biblical scholar for his criticisms of the text. He is also indebted to a number of able students (both among the clergy and laity in his home city) for valuable assistance in the revision of a number of chapters.

As an aid to the preparation of this volume many of the best known books of the modern critical school have been studied; and from some of these have been taken the excerpts that make up one of the chapters. This chapter tells its own remarkable story, and shows the character of many of the text-books and reference books used in our modern religious education. This volume is the first of its kind, and it will, doubtless, present to the Christian world a valuable revelation.

In connection with this book, the companion volume: the second edition of *The Modern Conflict Over The Bible* (350 pages—cloth) should be read. As a study of fundamental Christian Truth the latter is far more complete than this present volume. The enlarged edition is now coming from the press. The first edition of 25.000 copies was issued in March, 1918, more than half of which was donated to students and pastors.

If the reader believes that this literature should have a wide reading he is invited to furnish names to whom he would like to have it sent and a gift to cover the cost. It is hoped that some friends will provide for the sending of large numbers of these books to the professors and students in our institutions, and to others.

One of the largest book publishers in America desired to introduce to the Christian public this volume, and its companion volume, *The Modern Conflict Over The Bible;* but in order to make sure that these books will reach the source of our problem—the educational institutions—the Author decided to be his own publisher.

G. W. McPHERSON.

FOREWORD

THE extracts which compose a part of this volume may serve as a background, suggesting the imperative need for such a message as this. In taking the excerpts found in Chapter I, from a number of volumes that are representative of the New Theology and the radical criticism of the Bible, care has been taken not to do violence to the thought or injustice to the authors.

Doubtless there are many thoughtful persons to-day who could not be persuaded to accept the content of these extracts were they to hear it given from a public platform. With a desire to be just and charitable, those persons would say: "I am sorry but the speaker is exaggerating the whole situation. It surely cannot be as serious as he has represented. Some of these men I know personally; I heard them teach or preach, and entertained them in my home, and know that they are noble Christians, and could not write or teach such things about the Bible."

It is natural that personal friendship should play its part in hiding from many earnest people the situation in our institutions of learning. When some noted laymen, (not a few men and women of social and financial standing in New

York City) read *The Modern Conflict Over the Bible,* they said: "I cannot believe all this against those noble men in our institutions. This is a cheap harangue." Some were so shocked at the startling revelations that they indignantly declared "the author to be a sensationalist seeking notoriety, and not to be taken seriously, and may not be an authority on the matters of which he wrote. No, I do not believe his statements as to the teachings in our colleges, seminaries and churches."

It is because of the foregoing that these extracts are presented, in order that these readers and others may not rely upon the writer's statements, but get the facts from the critics' own works. Here then is the proof of our contention, which, when carefully read, will, doubtless, bring with it the needed vision. These are facts from the original sources and which cannot be gainsaid. It is the purpose, therefore, to indulge not in unproven charges, but to restrict the discussion in part to what the teachers of Modernism or the New Theology have to say about the Bible.

It is also not the purpose to impugn the motives, assail the characters, question the sincerity, or decry the scholarship of the advocates of the radical criticism, and the New Theology. It is believed that the scholarship of these men is, in some respects, equal to the scholarship of the conservative orthodox school. It is presumed that many of the critics are sincere in their work, and are endeavoring to do, what they understand to be, the will of God. While this is true, nevertheless, they are the victims of a false education, and of a great religious delusion, of which they themselves are unconscious.

The departure of the school of modern criticism from the fact of the inspiration and authority of the Bible, and from the belief in the Deity and eternal Sonship of the Lord Jesus Christ, is the result of the acceptance of a certain philosophy of the universe, in which they think they have found a new hypothesis or method of interpretation of the Bible. The objection to this method is, in part, that the critic exalts it above the thing he seeks to interpret. It should be made clear at the outset that this is one of our problems, namely: to convince the critic of his error in this regard, and thus induce him to renounce his false philosophy by which he attempts to interpret the Bible.

In opening a discussion of this nature it will be necessary to deal with those institutions where Modernism, or the New Theology is taught, the colleges and theological seminaries, and study the problem at its source. Numerous indictments have been made against our educational institutions. They have, in some cases, been charged with being anti-Christian, anti-Bible, anti-Church, and practically pagan. The atmosphere to-day is vibrant with these declarations. Conservatives have declared that in our schools there is rampant a subtle menace to Christianity. And so we must take up this statement, and, in the light of all the facts, see whether it is really true. This is the momentous question which we shall discuss in these pages.

That a vigorous denial is made by the advocates and friends of Modernism, the radical critics and their followers, is to be expected. These will probably reject the contention of this book; some of them mildly; while others will affirm that "our education is, on the whole, sane and healthful, pursues the true scientific method, and is not anti-Christian."

The question, therefore, to be decided is, which of these opposing parties is correct? It may not be too much to believe that this volume will help the reader to arrive at a reasonable and correct decision. It is patent that the forces of evangelical religion in America are rapidly losing faith in the value of the religious teachings in our universities. But on the other hand, we have it from Professor Harry Emerson Fosdick of Union Seminary, New York, in his article in The Atlantic Monthly of January, 1919, that "The intellectual classes, trying to think real thoughts about live issues, have gradually drifted away, until Christianity faces to-day, in the deflection of the universities, not from religion, but from the churches, a crisis of the first magnitude." Professor Fosdick may be taken to represent the radical school of critics of the Bible; and he says,

the universities are being alienated from the
churches because the latter are not thinking real
thoughts on live issues, such, for example, as the
newspapers and the magazines are doing. While,
on the other hand, we find the most intelligent
among the Christian people are declaring that the
churches are being deflected away from the universities; not because they would muzzle the true
teacher; but, rather, because the modern university has become a decidedly anti-Bible, anti-
Christian institution.

Thus we have the problem squarely before us.
Surely it is high time that this burning question,
which is threatening to work serious divisions in
the various Evangelical Bodies in America, be
cleared up; that all the facts be made known, in
order that the churches may be saved from needless and wicked disintegration and strife; and
that the educational institutions that are doing
helpful constructive work may be ably supported.

It is believed that the facts presented in the
following pages will convince the honest seeker
after truth that the claim of the churches, as
against the religious teaching in many of our
schools, is entirely justifiable. It may be assumed
that these authors from whose books the excerpts
are taken would hesitate to put in their publications all that they freely teach in classroom. It
should also be stated that these volumes are
typical of a large and rapidly increasing family
of similar publications which are flooding the

book market to-day; and that these are used as text-books and reference books in our institutions; and are viewed by many of our modern teachers as works of merit and authority.

The hope is cherished that this message will come to the modern teacher and advocate of the New Theology, whether he is in the pulpit, or pew, or university, as an honest, sincere, and helpful friend. *It is in the spirit of the utmost good-will that it is sent forth.*

This religious crisis of our time calls for sanity of judgment, painstaking investigation, and a decision of character to stand loyally for the Truth. But equally as important as these is that spirit of love to God and to men which alone can prepare the heart to form a charitable and correct judgment; and thus win, in this process, those who have lost the true vision of the Greatest of all teachers. God is Wisdom, Light, Love and Truth. Let us earnestly desire that these elements and powers may take possession of us as we study this message. If we lose God in our study, all is lost.

THE AUTHOR.

CONTENTS

CHAPTER I

EXCERPTS FROM TEXT BOOKS AND REFERENCE
BOOKS USED IN OUR INSTITUTIONS

1. *Systematic Theology and Christian Ethics,* by
   Gerald Birney Smith, Professor of Christian
   Theology in The Divinity School, Chicago University.

2. *New Testament History,* a study of the beginnings
   of Christianity, by Harris Franklin Rall, President and Professor of Systematic Theology, Denver University, Denver, Colorado.

3. *The Problems of Religion,* by Durant Drake, Professor in Vassar.

4. *The Old Testament in the Light of To-day,* by
   William Frederick Bade, Professor of Old Testament Literature and the Semitic Language in the
   Pacific Theological Seminary.

5. *Evolution and Christianity,* by Lyman Abbott.

6. *The History of Religion,* by E. Washburn Hopkins,
   Professor in Sanskrit and Comparative Philology,
   Yale University.

7. *The Religion of Israel,* by George A. Barton, Professor of Biblical Literature and Semitic Language in Bryn Mawr College.

8. *Protestant Thought,* by Arthur Cushman McGiffert,
   President, Union Theological Seminary, New
   York.

9. *The Ethics of Jesus and Social Progress,* by B. Gardner.

10. *The History of Religion,* by Allen Menzies.

11. *Theology of the Old Testament,* by A. B. Davidson.

12. *The Environment of Early Christianity,* by S. Angus.

13. *The Contribution of Critical Scholarship to Ministerial Efficiency,* by George Burman Foster, Professor of The Philosophy of Religion, University of Chicago, published in *A Guide to the Study of the Christian Religion.*

14. *The Shorter Bible,* by Professor Charles Foster Kent, Yale University.

Extracts from *Systematic Theology and Christian Ethics,* by Gerald Birney Smith, Professor Christian Theology, in the Divinity School, Chicago University.

(Numbers on the margin indicate the pages from which extracts have been taken.)

We have inherited the conception of Christianity as a perfect revelation of truth [as given in the Bible] which abides substantially unchanged from age to age. The theologian from this point of view, is not searching for truth, as are men 486 who deal with mere human science. His truth is given to him by revelation [in the Bible] and has only to be effectively expounded and interpreted [that is, applied to human life in each generation.] But he [the present-day theologian] as all his predecessors, would be expected to find the content of Christian truth already given in the Bible.

But what does the history of religious thinking reveal? Has the content of Christianity actually remained constant? 487 For example, do we take seriously to-day the biblical doctrine of demons? The fact that Christian theology has actually been developing and changing throughout its history comes into conflict with the theory of divinely authorized and unchangeable content of doctrine.

Many thinkers of our time feel that this inherited system [the Bible] does not do justice to the demands of living faith. There is a rapidly increasing number of loyal Christians, who 488 insist that religious beliefs must be large enough to include the truth of modern discovery as well as the truth of ancient Scripture.

We, like every generation, have inherited doctrines and ideals, but we have our own peculiar problems to face, and we must use our inheritance [the Bible] and, where necessary, 493 modify it, [the Bible] so as to meet these problems. In so far as our life differs from those of former generations our beliefs must differ.

When one has come to abandon animism, a theology [or teaching] which proclaims the necessity of dealing with spirits and devils is impossible. [Animism is defined by the Standard 511 Dictionary as: "The belief in the existence of spirit or soul as distinct from matter and of a spiritual world as distinguished from a material world."]

Originally it was expected that all followers of Jesus would live until he returned. It was only when death overtook some that the resurrection was discussed. To the query as to whether those who had died were to lose their rights in the Kingdom 539 the answer was given that the dead should have their bodies restored to them at the time of the great consummation [the Second Coming of Christ] so that they might participate in the great joys of the Kingdom. As time went on and the expected catastrophe [the resurrection and the Coming of Christ] did not take place, Christianity gradually developed the idea of heaven.

Extracts from *New Testament History, A Study of the Beginnings of Christianity*, by Harris Franklin Rall, President, and Professor of Systematic Theology, Denver University, Denver, Colorado.

We do not know much of these [mystery] religions [that are supposed to have come into the Roman Empire from Persia]. Of these mystery religions there were many kinds. . . . They were usually founded upon some story, the mystery, the tale of some god and of his life and death and coming to life again. . .
18 These religions were marked by ceremonies and sacraments. . . . The great thought was that of redemption. The great end was deliverance from evil, especially death, by means of union with the god. . . . Here are societies like the churches with sacraments of supper and baptism and the story of a dying and risen god. . . . [NOTE: While the author disclaims these religions as being Christian, yet the inference is that possibly Christianity borrowed some of their ideas.]

It is always to be remembered, however, that it is the char-
35 acter and life of Jesus which led us to believe in the virgin birth, and not the virgin birth which led us to believe in Jesus.

Such cases of demoniac healing were an undoubted part of Jesus' work. We cannot, of course be sure of all details. As
55 to Jesus' own conception [of these miracles] we cannot tell. So far as ordinary knowledge is concerned we find him elsewhere sharing the opinions of his time.

Jesus did not take from the Old Testament indifferently; he discriminated and chose. . . . There were large portions which he left wholly to one side. He set scripture against scripture. . . . He did not argue against the old. He simply let it slough off.

Neither the Old Testament nor the teachers of Jesus' day knew anything of a suffering Messiah.   11

Paul began his work on his own account. The mother church at Jerusalem gave him no credentials.   16

With the exception of Peter, it seemed that they [the leaders of the Church] were content to remain at Jerusalem, praying 19 and waiting for the heavens to open again and Christ to return.

Extracts from *Problems of Religion,* by Durant Drake, a text book that has been used in a certain Church college, reinstatement of which the senior class petitioned.

As later, in the case of Christ, legends of miraculous birth and many wonders grew up around his [Buddha's] memory and were devoutly believed. Indeed, the similarity between the lives of these two, the world's greatest teachers, and between the beliefs of subsequent ages about them, is in many ways striking. . . . Both inheriting the conceptions by means of which they taught. . . . Both holding out to men a way of salvation and peace, found that way in its fundamental aspects identical. . . . Both were in essence the message of a better 44 way of life, but little affected by speculation and involving allegiance to no creed. The Way of both teachers was the Way of love and purity and self-surrender. Both teachers inspired great personal loyalty and soon came to be thought of as semi-divine; as coming from heaven to save men; of both were many miracles and marvels told; and with the teaching of both was incorporated a mass of contemporary and subsequent speculation.

As for Jehovah, he was, it seems, originally a storm-god of
52 Mount Sinai. . . .Various Biblical allusions show us that his
home was long thought to be in the South. [NOTE: No references are given.]

56   The conception of Jehovah became ennobled until he grew
from just such a capricious and at times bloodthirsty tyrant.

But it [John's Gospel] is of little value in helping us to get
an idea of the real Jesus as he lived and taught on earth. The
Book was probably not intended to be taken as a literal record
of events, but as a dramatic picture illustrating and explaining
65 the author's conception of Jesus as the Logos or earthly Manifestation of God. The literary device by which speeches and
acts are attributed to Christ in accordance with what the
author conceived that he might have said and done, was not
uncommon or considered illegitimate in those days.

NOTE 3: The birth and infancy-stories with which the
66 first and third Gospels are now prefaced are later than the
bulk of those Gospels; together with the resurrection-stories
at the end, they are called by scholars " The Outer Envelope."

It is possible that Jesus expected when he went to Jerusalem,
69 at the time of the feast of the Passover, that Jehovah would
intervene there dramatically to vindicate him by investing
him with the Messianic powers.

Become skeptical, probably, of Jesus' pretensions, and with
70 that, of course, angry at his presumption . . . Judas betrayed
his secret claim to the Messiahship to the Priests.

We can guess the bitter doubt that found utterance in the
despairing cry, from the cross, "My God, My God, why hast
71 thou forsaken me." But he conquered his weakness, bowed
to the divine plan, and met his death serenely, a martyr to
his faith in his own destiny.

That Jesus should have shared this delusion, and especially that he should have believed himself the One destined by God to play the role of Messiah, may seem strange to us. 78

NOTE 4: The stories at the end of our Gospels are so late in origin, so confused and mutually contradictory, so out of line with Paul's allusions and with all inherent plausibility, that they must be pretty completely discounted. Paul shows 83 no knowledge of an empty tomb; Christ's resurrection in his thought is an emergence of his spirit from the region of the dead—a spiritual resurrection such as he expected for all the faithful, not a reanimation of the body and rising from the 84 grave; indeed, the whole discussion in I Cor. xv, is aimed against those who understood the resurrection to mean a raising of the dead body. . . . Jesus himself never predicted the emergence of his body from the grave.

Paul was not really a great thinker. 9

The traditional conception of Christendom has been that it is the only true faith and all others are false. . . . Such a 22 judgment we have now come to see, was a presumptuous and narrow conceit.

Jesus shared the ignorance of men, not only in his boyhood, but throughout his life. He knew presumably no science, knew little of the life and history of the world, shared the local 14 contemporary beliefs and hopes of his fellows, was possessed in the last months or years of his life by a passionate conviction which in its literal form can only be called a pathetic delusion.

Not merely inconsistent with one another, however, but 27 obviously untrue are many of the Biblical statements.

In the Buddhist Scriptures are many passages more truly 27 inspired than the less inspired parts of our Bible.

275   The familiar assertion attributed to the evangelist Moody, among others, that the Bible is "the Word of God from cover to cover," is one calculated to blur our perception of religious values and do incalculable mischief.

285   No single case of what would be clearly a miracle has ever been vouched for by such careful scientific observation as to leave no room for doubt of the facts.

287   The reign of the Bible miracles is doomed. . . .

292   But as certainly we must, in the present state of evidence, render a verdict of "Not proven." . . . From being a prop of faith, they [the miracles] have become a stumbling block in the way of faith.

Extracts from Wm. Frederick Bade's *The Old Testament in the Light of To-day.*

A reference book to be read in a Church college by Professor. . . Class in Bible, notes to be taken and given teacher.

XX   Needless to say, the conception of revelation that underlies this study regards it as an illumination from within, not as a communication from without; as an educative, not as an instructional process.

11   The moral criticism applied to the Old Testament by Jesus implies our right to employ textual, historical and philosophical criticism.

15   Again and again it will be found that the thing represented as an event or phenomenon in the natural world was really in its origin an inner fact of consciousness externalized and interpreted as a fact of the phenomenal world—an inevitable concession to primitive modes of thought and to the uncon-

scious demand for concreteness during the earlier stages of religion. The voice in the garden, the divine visitors at Mamre, the burning bush, the physical manifestations and thunderous deliverances on Mount Sinai, the tables of stone themselves, belong to the poetry, to the religious psychology of Israel's religion, not to the historical facts of its history.

Yet the editors selected, expurgated, and harmonized these traditions into a superficial unity, but there remain these telltale chips from blocks of primitive tradition rejected by compilers. It was a compiler who identified the Noah of the Flood 21 with the Noah of Viticulture. In the original traditions they were undoubtedly two persons. The story of Cain and Abel is only a torso.

As additional instances might be mentioned two legends, in one of which Jahveh wrestles with Jacob at the ford of the Jabbok, and in the other attempts to slay Moses at a lodging 58 place on his way to Egypt. In both stories Jahveh has undoubtedly taken the place of local night-demons.

In order to find a mate for Adam he [God] first engaged in a futile experiment with animals. [The author interprets scrip- 64 ture as saying this.]

To a modern mind such acts of caprice are unthinkable in connection with God. . . . But the writers of J and E [docu- 6 ments] did not hesitate to endow Jahveh with their own passionate natures.

Thus it happens through ignorance of the facts of Israel's moral development on the one hand, and a false view of revelation on the other, that deplorably crude and immoral ideas about God are still imparted as "the Word of God." The corrective lies in realizing that fact, that the prophets naïvely 16 attributed to God their own feelings and sentiments which naturally did not rise at all points superior to the moral and aesthetic limitations of their age.

281   It is not the institution but the repudiation of sacrifice that distinguishes the religion of Israel.

In the face of such evidence the assertion that "the Scriptures of the Old and New Testaments are without error or misstatements in their moral and spiritual teachings and record of historical facts, is to create that serious situation in which faith and truth part company.

308

From Lyman Abbott's *Evolution and Cristianity*.

The following extracts are from chapter "The Evolution of The Bible," also required to be read by classes in Bible in a certain college, notes taken, etc.:

He reads the story of the Fall with its tree, the fruit of which was to make man immortal . . . its weedless garden and its talking serpent and its death following sin. He learns again from science that death has existed in the world from the beginning, and must have existed, that the immortality of man's body is an impossible conception, and that all science tends more and more to the conclusion that man as an animal has been developed by gradual processes from a lower animal condition.

31

An infallible book is an impossible conception, and to-day no one really believes that our present Bible is such a book.

36

The History of Religion, by E. Washburn Hopkins, Professor in Sanskrit and Comparative Philology in Yale University.

The following extracts are taken from only two chapters XX and XXIV in a book of more than

600 pages. In the twentieth chapter alone the author, in speaking of matters of the gravest import, used thirty odd times the following terms: "perhaps," "inferable," "probably," "possibly," "we may suppose," "may have been," "it seems," "Adam may have," "and probably heritage," "were probably," "is supposed," "appear to have," "supposedly," etc., etc.:

The god of the Israelites was Yahweh [Jehovah], a spirit possibly belonging to many Semitic groups, more especially to the Midianites. He was the god of this people and came 41 from Hareh, the country of the Midianites.

Some think that the notion of unclean animals was brought from Egypt with the rite of circumcision. This rite was probably part of a tribal initiation ceremony.

It seems historically reasonable to believe that Moses, like Mohammed, united various tribes and made real an ideal not wholly unknown before, in that he gave Israel its jealous protecting national divinity.

Their religious value remain the same whether they ever existed or not.

We may imagine Abraham to have been a parallel to the heroes of cultur-myths found in other religions or a local god; yet the Patriarch, who is said to have come to Palestine via Haran, may have existed, though it was historically likely that he was an idolized hero.

The religion of Christ stands to Christianity somewhat as that of Buddha to Buddhism. In each, interpretation begotten of speculation embraced alien thought and bore hybrid de-

scendants, some harking back to original features, others far
552 removed from any likeness to the founder. In other regards
also the two religions are similar. As Buddha has been resolved
into a sun-myth so Jesus Christ has been explained as cosmic
truth in legendary form, a Gilgamesh or other divine hero. . . .
Finally, the life, temptation, miracles, parables, and even the
disciples of Jesus have been derived directly from Buddhism.
[This is an illustration of the modern apostasy in its most
brazen attempt to falsify history.]

His birth [Jesus'] . . . is not spoken of as a supernatural
event by . . . Jesus himself; nor by any of his disciples in
their conversation is it referred to as a proof of his divinity.
[NOTE: We wonder how the author knows all this . Does he
assume that we have a complete record of all the conversations
of Jesus' disciples, and of our Lord's own words? It is unfair
to argue from the silence of this or that book against the Deity
of Jesus Christ. Moreover, his disciples do testify to His deity
in their writings.]

Paul, before whose death, 63 A.D., the new religion had
557 spread over the Roman empire, was the founder of Christianity
in distinction from the religion of Jesus.

Converted by a Christophany, he [Paul] saw Christ ever
above the earth.

The Religion of Israel, by George A. Barton, Prof. of Biblical Literature and Semitic Language in Bryn Mawr College.

During all the early history the Hebrews continued to hold
this belief that every rock, tree, spring, or other natural object
173 was believed to be animated by spirits although the pre-emi-
nence of Yahweh and his jealousy tended to push the consciousness of other spirits into the background.

Apart from spirits . . . we hear of Cherubim (Gen. 3:24) who were, perhaps, the personified winds. While the seraphim appear to have been composite figures, it is probable that they 178 were really winged serpents (Isa. 6:1–7) for in Numbers 21:6 fiery seraphim are really fiery serpents.

It thus appears that before the exile the Hebrews did not entertain a belief in demons in the ordinary sense of the term. The innumerable spirits who were, they thought, the attendants of Yahweh were non-ethical in character. They might be sent by him on any sort of a mission. If the task assigned one of them was helpful to man, the spirit was good; if harmful to 179 man, he was evil. The prophet Amos, for example, was so thorough a monotheist that he had no room in his theology for a Satan. He believed that Yahweh did all that was done, whether good or bad.

The conception that angels were intermediaries between Yahweh and men became necessary because at this time the 181 Jews were coming to think of God as so exalted that he would not act like a man.

The way in which Satan is here made to stand apart from the other "sons of the gods" is the starting point of that later development which regarded him as a fallen angel.

Both the conception of ranks of angels and the tendency to name them may possibly, though not necessarily, have been 188 borrowed from the Persians.

Apocalypse is a form of literature by itself. It is quite distinct from prophecy, and developed in Israel only after 248 prophecy had died out.

The motive of the Babylonian Creation Epic may be said 251 to underlie most, if not all, apocalypse.

In the opinion of the writer it [the book of Daniel] consists of a series of tracts for the times written by at least three different men though they all lived and wrote during the three 255 years mentioned. They all professed to relate visions which had been granted to Daniel, an old patriarch. . . . Toward the end of three years some editor collected these tracts into one little book.

The apostles did not understand their Master's more spir-261 itual view, and confidently expected Jesus to return on the clouds of heaven.

The Apostle Paul, himself a product of the dispersion, had imbibed the allegorical method and, in order to read Christian meanings into the old Testament stories he employs it more than once—see Gal. 4:21-31; I Cor. 10:1-4. Through Paul 276 the method passed into the Christian Church, where it has persisted until our own time. By this method the whole sacrificial theology of evangelical Christianity is found by some in the book of Leviticus. This time-honored method with all its vagaries Christianity inherited from the dispersion.

Extracts from *Protestant Thought,* by Arthur Cushman McGiffert, President of Union Theological Seminary, New York.

But David Hume [the noted infidel] was really concerned primarily to destroy the apologetic value of miracles, and for 221 that purpose his argument was valid and has never been successfully refuted . . . against the apologetic position of the day Hume's argument was really final.

That the Christian revelation was given so late in the history of the world, and was brought to the knowledge of so small a portion of the human race; that it narrowed the conditions of salvation set up by natural religion, requiring things

in themselves morally indifferent, and thus closing the door
to many virtuous and noble men of all ages and nations; that
the Old Testament is full of inconsistencies, inaccuracies, bad
ethics, and bad theology; that even the New Testament is [2]
beset in less degree with the same difficulties; that the history of
Christianity and the traditional theology of the Church contains much that is contradicted by sound reason and morality
—all this was emphasized over and over again.

The Ethics of Jesus and Social Progress, by B. Gardner.

If the Church is simply an instrumentality whose purpose
is and always should be the enthronement of the spirit and
ideals of Jesus in the whole social order, we ought not to be [80]
neither alarmed nor surprised that in proportion as this purpose
is accomplished the sense of need of the Church should relatively [81]
decline.   [The Church, according to this, is a fading institution,
of less value than an ethicalized unregenerated mass, called
society.]

The History of Religion, by Allen Menzies.

We shall not divide religions into the true one, Christianity,
and the false ones all the rest.   No religion will be to us a mere [7]
superstition, nor shall we regard any as unguided by God.

Religion must reflect the ideals of the society in which it
exists; the needs which the society feels at the time must be
the burden of its prayers; its sacrifices must be such as the [16]
general sentiment allows; its gods, to retain the allegiance
of the community, must alter with time, and prove themselves
alive and in touch with the people.

The theory that man was originally civilized and humane,
and that it was by a fall, by a degeneracy from the earliest
conditions that the stage of savagery made its appearance, is [19]
now generally abandoned." [Yes, by Unitarians and the
radical critics.]

189 The inspiration of Jehovah appeared in early times in some--
what crude forms.   Bands of fervid devotees were seen, who
produced in themselves by dance and song ecstatic enthusiasm
in which they were thought to become organs of the deity.

Theology of the Old Testament, by A. B. Davidson.

22 [Says   New Testament writers misinterpreted the Old
Testament.]   It is admitted that the sense put by New Testament writers on much of the Old Testament is not the true
historical sense, that is, not the sense, which the original writers,
prophets, or wise men, had in mind.

358 The traditional explanation [of sacrifices] has been that the
victim was a *poena vicaria* for the sin of the offender.   And
it is probable that this idea did become attached to the sacrifice.
It is questionable, however, when other things are considered,
if it be found in the law.   [This seems to be an effort to eliminate the Atonement.]

The Environment of Early Christianity, by S. Angus.

4, 5 In our day we cannot dislocate history, as was possible a
generation ago.   The idea of evolution and progress has too
firmly laid hold of our minds.   The unity of mankind and the
unity of history are articles of faith.   History is now viewed
as an organism.   The student cannot without impunity dissever
Christianity from the fabric of its age. . . . The study of
comparative religions has given rise to a degree of tolerance,
and enabled us to appreciate God's gradual unfolding of his
purpose, and self-revelation to different ways of thinking.

The Contribution of Critical Scholarship to Ministerial Efficiency, by George Burman Foster, Professor of the Philosophy of Religion, Univer-

sity of Chicago, published in "A Guide to the Study of the Christian Religion."

The minister spoke [formerly] with authority to the consciences and hearts of men. There was an accent of positive conviction that could not be mistaken. Men were made to face the tables of stone, the cross and the great white throne. . . . What has been going on? The calling becomes a vocation. . . . The sacred calling is becoming de-supernaturalized and, in a sense, de-spiritualized. . . . But one sees in this great change the method of the evolutionary process fully illustrated. 734

Thus in principle—though not yet entirely in fact—the historic sacrament is gone . . . gone is the origin of the sermon on the Holy Ghost . . . the naïve and primitive trust in divine afflatus . . . More serious still, the divinity of his church, of the doctrines and morals of his sermons, of the Head of the church, of the specific God of this theology—these too are gone, and with them the old miraculous supernaturalism of regeneration and sanctification and perfection. What has taken the place of all this that once constituted the religious basis of the ministerial calling? In part technique, machinery, capital, especially organization. The church is not a temple but a "plant." The idea seems to be gaining favor that if men are fed and clothed and sheltered and washed and amused they will not need to be redeemed with the old terrible redemption. 735

The human spirit urged a new mightier protest against the "It is written" . . . therefore allowing and ever rejoicing in the moral and religious value of many a page, the biblical canon as such had no right to rule over man. Man was the book's judge; the book was not man's judge. The book must be measured by man's truth, man's conscience. 740

(The above is the clearest statement of Modernism the author has yet seen.)

The Shorter Bible, by Professor Charles Foster Kent, of Yale University.

The following is a part of an editorial that appeared in the last November number of *Our Hope,* by the Editor, Dr. A. C. Gaebelein, in which he makes a criticism of Professor Kent's *The Shorter Bible.*

Before us is a small volume recently published in New York City. It is "The Shorter Bible," covering the New Testament Scriptures. The Shorter Bible of the Old Testament is in preparation. The chief editor of this production is Professor Charles Foster Kent of Yale University, one of the leading destructive critics and echoman of this German-made infidelity in our country.

We notice the contents of this "Shorter Bible" first. He has rearranged the record of the synoptic Gospels under seven divisions: 1. The universal significance of Jesus' birth. 2. The life of Jesus. 3. The Master teacher and his disciples. 4. God and Man. 5. Man and Society. 6. Man and his neighbor. 7. The Essentials of true happiness. Different parts of the three Gospels are taken out of their divinely given places and jumbled together to suit the purpose of this critic. In looking over these seven parts, we find that the name "Jesus" is used 34 times, but not once is He called Lord. It is constantly his earthly name; never once is He designated as the Lord. The Gospel of John is put at the close of this Shorter Bible, though a few passages are quoted under some of the above sections.

The way the Epistles are treated give conclusive evidence what spirit is behind this attempt to introduce a Shorter Bible. We given an illustration. Here is Romans III; 19–28—that sublime passage containing such vital truth. The whole passage is given in this Shorter Bible except two verses. The verses omitted are the twenty-fifth and twenty-sixth, the most important: "Whom God hath set forth to be a propitiation through faith in His blood to declare His righteousness for the remission of sins that are past through the forbearance of God, to declare I say His righteousness, that He might be just and the justifier of Him who believeth in Jesus." What reason can there be given to multilate this great passage by leaving out the statement without which the passage has no meaning whatever? Perhaps Professor Charles Foster Kent and his assistants have little use for blood, for the substitutionary sacrifice of the Lord Jesus Christ. Not believing it, it is as much as possible eliminated in this Shorter Bible.

And here are a few more omissions. Not a word of the raising of Lazarus from the dead. Matt. xii: 38–42 is quoted, except verse 40, "For as Jonah was three days and three nights in the whale's belly, so shall the Son of Man be three days and three nights in the heart of the earth." Of course you could not expect Prof. Charles Foster Kent of the great Yale University to believe in the history of Jonah! So out it has to go, though He who is the Truth spoke these words. The entire 24th chapter of Matthew is also put out, nor is one of the greatest revelations of the whole Bible permitted to have a place in the Shorter Bible. We have reference to I Thess. iv; 13–18. Not a single word is given of this unique revelation concerning the Coming of the Lord.

But enough of it. No true believer needs to be told that spirit is behind such a deliberate attempt at mutilation of the Word of God. It is the same work which wicked King Jehoiakim did when with a pen-knife he cut the roll on which the Word was written and cast it into the fire. And Prof. Kent should know as professor of Biblical literature of Yale University, that King Jehoiakim was buried with the burial of an ass (Jer. xxii:19). Woe unto the man who touches God's living, holy Word and takes away his truth. But what another evidence of the fast approaching predicted apostasy!

PRACTICAL OBSERVATIONS

The astounding thing is that these critics can pose as Christians, that they are permitted to retain membership in churches, and occupy places of responsibility in educational institutions. That the Boards permit such men to serve as teachers proves that either the officials are in sympathy with this critical propaganda or that they are asleep and know nothing of what is being taught in their institutions. In either case it would appear that such officers are hardly qualified to serve in their positions of honor and responsibility.

It should be stated in the utmost candor that these excerpts which comprise this chapter contain but few statements of fact regarding the Bible. They are too dishonest with history, as may be seen by intelligent students, to merit a categorical reply. These writers reveal a peculiar animus toward the facts of sacred history.

One of the serious things about the campaign is that our boys and girls will inevitably come to accept similar views of the Bible, and thus become allied with the forces of Modernism and practical infidelity. How long can such a method of education continue and America remain even nominally Christian?

CHAPTER II

CORRESPONDENCE WITH PRESIDENTS OF OUR EDUCATIONAL INSTITUTIONS

PROBABLY few persons have been so favored as the author in learning the opinions of many of the most noted educators in America regarding the religious problems in the thinking of university men.

The study of 211 letters, which have been received from as many noted educators, furnish in some respect a liberal education. It is with sincere gratitude that reference is made to those distinguished men who, in the midst of their numerous duties, have taken such pains to express themselves so frankly and honestly on the great matters under consideration. Doubtless, aside from the parents of the students, the Presidents of our institutions are most interested in the moral and spiritual welfare of those committed to their instruction and guidance. Only a small per centum of those who replied to the letter sent out, failed to show deep interest in the highest welfare of the students. Some of the letters received are so fatherly and tender, deeply spiritual and touching in character, that it is a real pleasure and benediction to read them.

Following is the letter sent by the author:

My Dear Sir:

As you may not know the writer, perhaps this letter-head of The Old-Tent Evangel Committee of New York will serve as an introduction. I have been Superintendent of the above union work for seventeen years.

Occasionally I address students and have become much interested in them. From personal interviews with students I have learned that there is a growing problem in their thinking. As far as I have been able to learn I find that the problem has arisen over the teaching of science, philosophy, and theology, from the standpoint of evolution, and the supposed conflict of science with the teaching of Genesis and the miraculous element in the Bible as history; and consequently the difficulty for the student to relate his thinking in the realm of religion with his thinking in the realm of science and philosophy.

How general this problem is in the minds of the students I have no way of knowing. I am, therefore, taking the liberty to write to the heads of some of our institutions asking if they will kindly favor me with their personal opinions as to this matter. I know that this is asking much but I assure you that your reply would be greatly appreciated. Your name will be considered strictly confidential.

I know you are a busy man, and if you should feel somewhat out of touch with the matter about which I am seeking information, would you be so kind as to refer my letter to some one who is qualified to give a reply.

In order to make my thought as clear as possible, may I ask for a reply to the following questions?

1. Have the students in your institution generally accepted as fact the philosophy of evolution?

2. If so, have they as result rejected the teaching of Genesis as to the creation and the miraculous element generally in the Bible as historical?

3. Are the new theology and the higher criticism point of view taught by any of the teachers in your institution,

and if so to what extent have the students accepted this teaching as authoritative?

Thanking you for your reply, I beg to remain,

Sincerely yours,

G. W. McPHERSON.

The replies to the above letter are classified as follows:

Baptist	45	Lutheran	7
Methodist	39	Disciples	9
Presbyterian	19	United Presbyterian	6
Dutch Reformed	5	Congregational	22
Episcopalian	5	United Brethren	4
	Miscellaneous	50	

GENERAL ANALYSIS

It is exceedingly difficult to make an exact analysis and classification of the replies received. Probably it would be somewhat unjust to the educational institutions to attempt this. It is, of course, possible that in some cases, at least, the President or the Professor whom he asked to write for him, may not have been fully qualified to speak for all the students, and, at best, his statement should be taken rather loosely, especially when it deals with the faith of the entire student body. While making all necessary allowance for this, nevertheless, the replies received do reveal a state of mind on the part of the teacher that is illuminating and interesting.

Some of the letters are exceedingly frank, others are quite evasive, some deal with the question of evolution wholly, others with evolution, religion and socialism; while others discuss the New Theology; and still others write about theology and modern evangelism. Some of these friends declared that they never heard of the New Theology, others differed widely as to the value of Higher Criticism. A few showed a spirit of antagonism to the so-called sensational evangelist, while others told with enthusiasm of the great evangelistic work in their institutions. One College President said that all the students in his institution had made a confession of faith in Jesus Christ as his personal Saviour, while a few revealed that they were somewhat skeptical as to what is termed conversion, and that the only hope for humanity is found in the slow but ever upward ascent of man under the beneficent law of evolution. A *striking tendency* is noted in many cases to avoid the use of strictly Christian terms, and instead, to use terms less meaningful as, for example, ideal in place of Christ, the vague, loose term religion in place of Christianity, and ethical ideals rather than any terms that would reveal the Supernatural or any special revelation of God as given in the Bible. ''The stronger students are devoted to the Christian ideals,'' illustrates the tendency to substitute weak terms in place of strong, definite, meaningful, Christian, and more personal terms.

EVOLUTION.

As to evolution the majority teach it, but a respectable minority took pains to state that evolution is not taught as fact in their institutions. Regarding this philosophy, there is in evidence a great variety of opinion. A few stated that they do not permit evolution to be taught in their institutions, nor any of the methods of study known as the radical criticism of the Bible. It was noticed from some of the letters that the war had given a decided check to the tendency, during the last few decades, to teach in a dogmatic fashion the rationalistic philosophies generally. In a few colleges all such teaching has been prohibited, and in some cases this type of teacher has been dismissed. It is noted that this also is true to some extent of the Theological Seminaries. In one of the latter the Professors in theology and homiletics have been compelled to resign, and other teachers of the critical school are known to be decidedly uneasy. It is a pleasure to note this evidence of real reform in certain institutions, rare though it be.

Evolution, however, is still the great working hypothesis in most of our institutions, especially in the Northern States. In the South a different atmosphere is in evidence. On the whole our education appears in the South to be more safe and sane than in the North. In New England, for example, a circle could be drawn around this geographical section and across it written "German Kultur," for in these parts the radical criticism, rationalism, and skepticism, abetted always by Unitarianism, have made their mark. Evolution is almost a college god in New England, and he is greatly admired in his saints. The note of positive faith and religious authority seem to be lacking in the letters from this section. Jesus Christ is not in them exalted as the only Master and Lord, in the sense in which he is viewed in many other parts of America; with the exception of a few Preparatory Schools as, for example, The New London Academy in New Hampshire, which is one of the institutions worthy of high praise. New England Unitarianism is a warm friend of the criticism of the Bible, and its influence is felt, not only in the Colleges that are classed as orthodox, but also in the Theological Seminaries in those parts. The following quotation is from a letter received from a Theological Seminary in the heart of New England—"*The Hub.*":

The questions which you ask refer to a state of things which seem in the past. The philosophy of evolution, the new theology, and the higher criticism have become a part of our ordinary thinking, like the law of gravitation."

Few educators outside of New England, so far as they expressed an opinion on these matters, seem to be in full sympathy with the above opinion. The majority appear to feel that these great questions are still of vital interest, and are far from settled. When we come to the South and far Southwest, and parts of the West and far West, we find a more cheery, optimistic, enthusiastic and religious note, though there are centers in the East and Central West and far West as radical as New England.

Here is a letter from one of the conservative, yet progressive Theological Seminaries in the Central West; The Baptist Theological Seminary in Kansas City:

To your questions I would answer:

1. Our students have not "generally accepted as fact the philosophy of evolution." I doubt if any one of them has. Probably most of them who have particulary grappled with the problem would say that the history of the globe shows that God has pursued a method of *development*, but they would deny *in toto*, as all their teachers do, that any process of materialistic or naturalistic evolution accounts, or could account, for the physical, mental, moral, or spiritual universe as we see it to-day. Hence,

2. They do not in any sense "reject the teaching of Genesis as to the creation, or the miraculous element generally in the Bible as historical." Wherever the Bible, fairly interpreted, declares a miracle to have been performed, they accept the miracle as historical, because at the root of their thinking lies belief in a personal God, immanent, it is true, in His universe, but also transcendant, and so able and willing to control and supplement, if necessary, the usual methods of his working, by special outputs of power, miracles, to be precise. In their view, both miracle and prophecy, as well as special providence, are within the range of both the divine power and the divine wisdom, and are therefore not only possible but inevitable in the relations of a God of grace with a world of spiritual beings who need saving.

3. Neither the "new theology," nor what is usually, but

erroneously, called "the higher criticism point of view," is taught by any of our teachers. We believe in a sound and thorough Biblical criticism, using all the light obtainable from every source of real light, history, grammar, lexicography, etc., etc. The fair and honest use of these methods confirms us in the conviction that the Bible not only contains, but is, the veritable word of God, inspired, infallible, in every way veracious. At every point of debate with the divisive criticism, we hold the integrity of The Bible; the Mosaic authorship of the Pentateuch, the unity of the whole Isaiah, the verity of Daniel, the apostolic authorship of the Fourth Gospel, etc., etc. Needless to say, we teach the deity of Jesus, the vicarious atonement, the fact of the new birth, and the eternal difference in the unending destinies of the penitent and the impenitent. As far as I know we have not one student who is not in accord with our position, both in Biblical criticism and in doctrine.

The Seminary flies at its masthead that statement of Baptist doctrinal belief known as the "New Hampshire Confession."

Fraternally yours,

P. W. Crannell,
President.

The following is the reply from Wheaton College, Illinois, which stands four square for all the great fundamentals of the Christian Faith:

"Thank you for your kind note of November 20th. I reply hastily, but I trust fully to your inquiries.

In the first place, I do not know of any of our students who accept the philosophy of evolution; second, I think that all of our students believe the teaching of Genesis as to creation and that miracles recorded in the Bible are true; third, we do not knowingly permit any of our teachers to hold or teach views which are called the new theology and the higher criticism. Of course, I cannot say that none of them do believe the vagaries which masquerade under these titles, but so far as I have the knowledge the statements above made are true.

Personally I may say that I believe that the doctrine of evolution properly understood is infidel and atheistic. I have the satisfaction, however, of believing that many persons who call themselves evolutionists do not know what the word means.

Faithfully yours,

CHARLES A. BLANCHARD,

President.

Here is a letter written by one of the noted men in a certain well-known college. It will give a clear idea of the vast problem which is found in modern education as a result of the teaching of evolution. It should be stated that the definition of evolution, as given in this communication, is far from adequate:

MY DEAR MR. McPHERSON:

Your letter of the 20th inst. to President . . . has been turned over to me for an answer. It is a pleasure to write you concerning the problems you suggest. You touch one of the real problems in college teaching these days and one which more of our religious leaders should interest themselves in. Students as well as all thoughtful people find that there are differences between the doctrines and teachings of the pulpit and those of the philosophical, scientific and religious college teachers to-day. The beginnings of these differences is, however, in our High Schools and Preparatory Schools rather than in the colleges, though the matter comes back, of course, to the colleges, since these teachers are college men and women.

First, as to the doctrine of evolution. I suppose that every thoughtful, well-read man to-day considers himself, and that rightly, an evolutionist? The theory of evolution rigidly defined states simply that the present is the legitimate child of the past and will be the mother of the future. It is the theory which tries to see the universe as an organic whole, in action and moving eternally forward. It is simply the idea in the word Universe stated in organic form. However, having said this we meet at once at least three schools of evolutionists. These are the idealists, the materialists, and the go-betweens. The idealists insist that the essence of the universe is spirit, that personality is the chief thing, a purpose controls in all, and progress is towards a divine goal. The materialistic, including such thinkers as Haeckel, and Crampton of Columbia, see the original stuff as material, the evolution as the out-working of merely natural laws and the end "A purposeless continuity of ceaseless activity." The go-betweens are repre-sented by Bergson who tries to straddle and find the original stuff in God—Substance. Like all such, he thinks he leans to the spiritual side, but does not leave his readers with this impression.

Naturally in every educational institution there are repre-sentatives of all three schools. Where the materialists hold sway there is little chance for the Bible getting anything like a fair hearing. It is, however, interesting to hear these men rule out of court the miraculous and then in the next breath declare that the facts of evolution reveal the greatest miracles of history. I should say from a rather extended study of this science-philosophy that such teachers are more dog-matic than any church preacher could hope to be and in the end they simply steal the thunder of their supposed antagonists. I would also say that this teaching does not hold sway here. It is my pleasure to lead Chapel every morning and preach the college sermon at least two Sundays a month and to find that the spiritual view of this universe in which a just, righteous, and holy God rules and unfolds His eternal purpose finds a welcome and hearty response.

The following letter is of such a character that it is given in full:

Southwestern Baptist Theological Seminary,
Fort Worth, Texas,
November 28, 1918.

DEAR BROTHER:

Yours of the 20th inquiring concerning certain matters in the Southwestern Seminary to hand. I will answer your questions.

1. Have the students in your institution generally accepted as a fact the philosophy of evolution?

Answer: In a general sense, yes, as it applies to the physical world; but we do not accept it in its extreme application.

2. If so, have they as a result rejected the teachings of Genesis as to the creation and the miraculous element generally in the Bible, as historic?

Answer: No, the faculty and students of this institution accept the Genesis record of creation and the miraculous element in the Bible. We would not cut out one syllable in God's Book.

3. Are the new theology and the high criticism point of view taught by any of the teachers in your institution; and, if so, to what extent have the students accepted this teaching as authoritative?

Answer: We reject the whole ultra-criticism position as unsound and infidelic. I would at once dismiss any teacher that taught the heresies of ultra-criticism. We believe that the whole thing is bottomed on German Kultur. We accept and appreciate the value of historical criticism, but do not to the destruction of the binding authority of God's word.

This institution is the second largest seminary in the world, with an enrollment of more than 350. It takes the old, orthodox view of theology, set on fire by the Holy Ghost. We have taken our stand, and "having done all" we expect to stand.

Yours fraternally.

L. R. SCARBOROUGH,
President.

Here is a cheerful note from the Southwest:

Oklahoma University.

MY DEAR BROTHER McPHERSON:

Your letter of November 20th addressed to me has been received, and greatly appreciated. I have kept in touch with you for several years through the press and by reading your productions. . . .

Four years ago, I was honored with the Presidency of our new Baptist College of Oklahoma. On accepting the position, I gave the Board to understand that no New Theology man, nor modern evolutionist, nor destructive critic, nor the materialistic thinker could ever hold a chair in this institution. Every member of our faculty and members of the college of fine arts all belong to the class who deny the philosophy of evolution, and hold to the miraculous in the scriptures and that Genesis is historically true. Since our faculty is sound, we have no trouble with the student body.

We have the annual college revival of the old evangelical type, and the students are reached and go home converted. Our ministerial students are of the soul winning, missionary type.

. . . Do not think for one minute that we have a weak faculty, for we have one of the strongest in scholarship and experience in the southwest. . . .

I beg to remain,

Yours very truly,

F. M. MASTERS,

President.

The following letter is from Rev. Shailer Mathews, D.D., Dean of the Divinity School, Chicago University; published by permission of Dr. Mathews:

MY DEAR MR. McPHERSON:

In reply to your circular letter of November 20th, I would say that it is quite impossible to know what something like 10,000 students believe individually. In so far as I come in contact with them, however, I find that a vast number of religious doubts are caused by the narrow and unintelligent religious teaching which they have received before coming to the University. When they are introduced into the world of research and experimental fact they find it necessary to question these earlier beliefs. It is a critical moment in their lives and we do everything we can to help them into a faith which is consistent with the facts of the universe as we are coming to know them. My own experience is like that of the late Henry Drummond, that most skepticism in college students is due to the *extreme teaching* of the inspiration of the Bible.

In particular as regards your questions, with the above reservation, I would say:

1. The probability is that the *more intelligent students* of the University have accepted the fact of *evolution* without committing themselves to any particular formulation as final. To do less than this would be to *stultify* themselves.

2. No one can answer so general a question which concerns fact and not individuals' opinions about other people's opinions.

3. I do not know what you mean by "the new theology." So far as I know there is no single system. As for higher criticism, we not only use it in the study of the Bible, but we believe any person who does not use it is not studying the Bible wisely or efficiently. I do not know what you yourself mean by the term "higher criticism." Your questions seem to imply that you were using it as if it were a body of teachings rather than a method of investigation.

In my opinion the sooner evangelists and ministers preach a theology which is consistent with the actual facts of the universe, the better it will be for all parties concerned. One of the greatest dangers which beset the church to-day is the preaching of *premillenarian irrationalities* and the refusal of the religious teachers to see that if doctrine is to be true, it must be based upon facts rather than upon *ecclesiastical* authority.

> Yours very sincerely,
> SHAILER MATHEWS.

Three statements stand out in the above letter.

1. Strong belief in the inspiration of the Bible produces skepticism.

2.   One of the greatest dangers which beset the church to-day is the preaching that Jesus is coming before the millennium.

3.   Doctrine to be true must be based on fact and not on ecclesiastical authority—by which Dr. Mathews probably means the authority of the Bible. Dr. Mathews' reference to Henry Drummond reminds us of what Spurgeon said in commenting on Drummond's book: "I have read the book and whether it be a good book or bad book I cannot tell." A year later he said: "Since writing the above I have read Drummond's book again, and again I say, whether it be a good book or bad book I cannot tell; but I think it is a bad book."

With few exceptions the above letters are a stimulus to Christian faith. The more radical type have been purposely omitted. The conclusion should not be drawn, however, that these magnificent declarations illustrate the prevailing spirit in modern education. They are rather the exception. Radicalism is rampant in most of the universities in the Northern states. In nearly every center of population the New Theology is strongly intrenched, though probably outside the larger cities, New England is where it is most in evidence. Students graduate from these institutions to-day, as did Americans in former years from the German Universities, to take up the profession of teaching and preaching in every part of this broad land. Here then we find America's greatest peril and political and religious problem.

AN INTELLIGENT DEFENSE

For the forty per cent. of those who communicated with the author, and who have not bowed the knee to "German Kultur," or modern skepticism, we should be thankful. The hour has come when the sixty per cent. should be either led to repentance or dismissed as teachers. It is a pleasure to note that some of those who are loyal to the Bible as the Word of God, are among the ablest scholars and religious thinkers in the world. Of course the greatest scholars in all periods of the Christian era have been on the side of the Bible. It is usually the shallow thinkers who oppose the authority of this mighty Book. It would be of interest to take a brief glance and recall the names of a few of the vast host of Christian scholars and thinkers the world over, in our institutions and out, as teachers, preachers, and others, who are loyal to God and His Word.

Mention need only be made of a few as suggestive of the noble body of the thousands whose names would fill a large book. Think of those grand men in Scotland: Professor James Orr, Dr.

Thomas Whitelaw; and in England: Bishop H. G. G. Moule, Dr. G. Campbell Morgan, Dr. F. B. Meyer, Dr. Prebendary Webb-Peploe; and in the United States: Dr. Franklin Johnson, Bishop John L. Nuelsen, Dr. C. I. Scofield, Dr. Charles R. Erdman, Dr. R. A. Torrey, Dr. James M. Gray, Dr. Sylvester Burnham, Dr. George Frederick Wright, Dr. M. G. Kyle, Professor Townsend; and in Canada: Dr. William Caven, Mr. Dyson Hague, Dr. W. M. Griffith Thomas, Mr. John McNichol; and many others, whose names might be mentioned, and who, with these, are among the noblest sons of the Christian Church. All this vast host are striving with voice and pen to spread abroad the glorious Revelation of God's saving love, as made known in the book we call the Bible. These leaders represent a mighty army, probably seventy-five per cent. of Protestantism, who are loyal to fundamental Christianity. Let men follow in their steps, for they are "the light of the world."

But over against this noble type of scholars and saints are pitted the growing school of skepticism in our educational institutions, and in some of our pulpits. Among these are not found great prophets of God, no giant preachers, no flaming evangelists, but a cold, intellectual, critical type. Many of these apostles of "German Kultur" however, are no novices. To refute and expose their false reasoning and theories call for reason and facts, and not mere rhetoric. Calling these critics names as, "religious snoops," "traitors," "fakirs," "hypocrites," "infidels," etc., will not yield good results. We must match brains with brains; we must get deeper inside the Bible; we must show these men their errors from the Book itself. They can be defeated. Indeed, they are now defeated; but they have not as yet awakened to the fact. Many of them seem to be as those described by our Lord in Mark 8:18: "Having eyes, see not, and having ears, hear not." They pit science against Revelation, but they do not stop to think that whenever in the past the critics pitted science against the Bible time proved by the spade, and in other ways, that the scientist was wrong and the Bible right. They are defeated to-day, and the Christian can be assured of the final issue. Our duty is to expose and bring these false teachers to realize the fact that they cannot remain in our institutions to destroy our most precious treasure—our Christian faith. They are as stated elsewhere, the victims of a false education, of a great religious delusion, though most of these critics are men of noble character and exalted purpose. They are blindly groping about for the Light.

CHAPTER III

MODERNISM IN AMERICA

THE great war has been fought and won and now the whole world stands at a time in history of partial cleavage from the past and facing a new and uncertain future.

Fear seems to have gripped the hearts of men everywhere as in a vise. Here and there are found some professed optimists who sing and whistle and declare that the world is facing a near millennium. It is evident, however, that even these professed enthusiasts reveal an undertone of uncertainty regarding our future as a nation. This is especially true of to-day as we enter upon a new era of readjustment and reconstruction.

The question that is pressing upon America from every quarter is, What of the future? Doubtless a new social order, a new America is coming, but with what material shall it be constructed?

The American soldiers have done their part, they have made their great contribution toward winning the war—the victory for international liberty and justice—and in this unsurpassed achievement they have, with our heroic Allies, won for mankind untold blessings and for the Western Nations undying fame.

One by one the enemies of liberty have been beaten to the ground, until the last and most malevolent of them all has surrendered. And now from all this sacrifice, this precious blood so gloriously and freely shed by the freer peoples of the world, far-reaching results must follow. It is ours to say to-day in the words of the immortal Lincoln: "These men shall not have died in vain."

It should not be forgotten, however, regarding all these matters that are looming up before the world for decision, that the modern New Theology, or Modernism, must have an important bearing.

But what do we mean by Modernism? What have religious teachings to do with the safeguarding of nations? Is there any kinship between the New Theology, for example, and the recent war? Is any such affirmative proposition unreasonable, far-fetched, a mere phase of wartime psychology, that sees things out of their true proportions and relations, an illustration of a perverted judgment, or religious narrowness and bigotry?

To many who do not understand the new religous movement, or better, the modern anti-Christian movement, and its effect upon institutions, individuals and nations, it may appear in itself to be harmless, even helpful, an expression of progress and love for the Truth; whereas, it is a ship adrift upon a dark and raging sea, without chart and compass, whose mariners strive in the stress of the storm and the darkness of the night to get a glimpse of the North Star.

This contention is not a strange mirage or figment of the imagination. We are not pursuing the rainbow for the elusive and fabled pot of gold, but rather we are uncovering a most serious matter, and that ought to be, by way of solemn instruction and warning, to the religious world, if properly used, a fissure-vein, the farther we advance the richer the nuggets. Let prejudices be suppressed and the discussion followed to the end. We shall show a real menace, a colossal evil that has spread its blight over many parts of the earth, a subtle system of false criticism of the Bible, a religion of doubt and respectable infidelity, all of which comes in the name of scholarship, and under the guise of piety, and that has at last manifested its true nature in church and college, and also in the awful panoply of war. It is because of the far-reaching influence of these facts, and the serious lesson they convey to the Christian world that we have decided to expose this anti-Christian propaganda in our modern education.

With the clear moral vision that has come, we would indeed be recreant to our high trust if we did not play the part of true sons of God and His Kingdom, and point out to America and to the world, in unmistakable fashion the results of Modernism in education, both secular and religious.

"Lying between New Brunswick, Nova Scotia, and the Maine coast, there is a body of water known as the Bay of Fundy. The conformation of this land is of such character that, whereas the ordinary tide rises betwen five and six feet during each twelve hours, the tide in this bay rises generally to twenty-five and thirty feet, and at its head sixty and seventy feet. People who have seen this tide come in give a wonderful description of it. The crest of the wave may be seen as far as the eye can reach, and it tumbles in a perfect fury as it rushes toward the head of the bay, enveloping everything in its course. Woe to the hapless man or beast that is caught on the sand banks! Woe to the unwary fisherman who may have lingered too long in the shallows! For the wave knows no mercy, and sweeps all to destruction except those who know the perils of the flowing tide and have sought safety."

This is a picture of the rising tide of an anti-Christian philosophy in American institutions, and its perils. We have not been invaded by an army, but the enemy has come in like a flood upon us and has captured many of our educational institutions.

WAS IT GERMAN PROPAGANDA?

The campaign of Modernism is believed by many to have been part of a deep laid plan to Germanize American education, and thus neutralize us in the day when the Teuton would strike for the mastery of the world. The proposition may appear reasonable, for a similar education in religion and philosophy would tend toward creating a powerful bond of sympathy between peoples, even though it be a false religion and philosophy. We are disinclined, however, to accept this explanation.

America has largely been an evangelical Protestant nation. Even yet, notwithstanding the increase in population, at least seventy-five per cent. are Protestant in religious faith. Germany well knew what a powerful factor this large element is in shaping our foreign policies, how this moral force fought here on this continent the greatest war of history, prior to the recent European struggle, and that to win the sympathy, the good-will of Protestant America, would be a master stroke. Consequently, it is claimed that Germany set about to accomplish this object in various ways, chief of which was to Germanize our education. We know that the ambition of the Teuton to master the world was boundless; nevertheless, we are not certain that Germany planned to capture American education and make it in content essentially German, though Mr. Arthur

N. Davis, the Kaiser's dentist, in his book—*The Kaiser as I Know Him*—argues to the contrary.

Whether this was or was not the aim of Germany, there seems to be a real friendship on the part of the New Theology advocates for German religious opinions. In many of our universities the atmosphere, even in theology, seems to be decidedly German; by which we mean to say, it is an atmosphere of criticism and doubt.

THE SPREAD OF MODERNISM

The New Theology point of view of the Bible and religion has long since traveled beyond its native soil. To-day it is found in Great Britain, Canada, the United States, Australia, New Zealand, Japan, some of the mission fields—in fact, it is getting a footing in nearly every center of education the world around. Of all the countries, however, outside of Germany, America is where this subtle system of criticism, doubt and opposition to a Revealed Religion has done its most destructive work.

For nearly two generations this teaching has been flourishing here in many of our institutions of learning. In all the Northern, but especially in the New England States, it has had much to do in moulding religious opinion. Few of our institutions in the North have escaped its blight. It is taught, with few exceptions, in our colleges, universities, divinity schools, normal schools, and even in some of our high schools. It may be found in the files of every newspaper, in our weekly and monthly magazines, in every library, in not a few of the Christian pulpits, as it is compromised with by many of the publishers and editors of religious literature, and embraced by thoughtless, skeptical, and superficial Bible students, and others, in many walks of life.

HOW IT CAME TO AMERICA

How did such a system of criticism and subtle antagonism to the Bible, as a Supernatural Revelation, find its way to America, and what has been the secret of its spread among the people? The answer is at hand. During the last four decades not a few of our college men took postgraduate work in the German universities, in order to equip themselves for teaching at home. In these institutions they were instructed by the noted teachers of rationalism, materialistic evolution, and the destructive criticism of the Bible, with the result that they accepted these principles and philosophies that later set Europe and the world on fire. Our splendid young men were taught in Germany to look upon the great historic facts of the Bible as largely fable, tradition and superstition, fit only for the people of a dead and far gone past. They were instructed to view the doctrines of Creation and the Fall, as recorded in Genesis, as legendary, poetry, and of the Virgin Birth, Deity, Resurrection of Christ, and redemption through his blood, as mythological, though with reverence, tolerance and patience, but withal with intellectual contempt.

And what has been the result? Our students, in many cases, returned to sneer at "Sunday-School religion," and the great facts of Christianity. Of course to be "learned," they too must teach here at home, as did their masters at Heidelberg, the new doctrines.

Then again, German books on theology, psychology, philosophy and science were translated and scattered broadcast over the world. No instructor was supposed to be well informed who did not bow to their authority. Thus by the work of our own students, and by books of German authorship, which are found in every university library and classroom, either as text-books or reference books, the anti-Bible Modernism has been popularized and entrenched in America. The respectable swarm of false theories made weighty and acceptable by the influence of the Prussian Universities has taken root in many parts of this Republic.

A SUBTLE DANGER

America is slowly waking to the fact that we have been invaded by a form of respectable infidelity the peril of which lies, in part, in its subtlety, its apparent and professed innocence and harmlessness—for it announces itself as "broad and unbiased," "a seeker after the Truth," "a lover of Christian unity," while at the same time referring to those who oppose it as "narrow-minded," "bigoted," "ignorant," etc.

The New Theology has learned the art of misrepresenting history. It can so influence our young men and women in our institutions of learning that they return to their friends to deny everything they had formerly believed as sacred and vital to their faith. The Bible is to them no longer the Word of God and authority. They are themselves the only authority. They view the past, with its prophets, saints and martyrs with some toleration, but withal with pity mingled with contempt; while the present they worship. They laugh at the old-fashioned out-of-date folks who cherish faith in the "obsolete doctrines."

Herein then lies the danger of Modernism: It is a system of blind optimism that greets the world with a laugh; that wears the smile of an angel, the dignified robes of the university and of religion; but like an old master's impersonation of sin, it would not be unkind to say: "it carries a danger in its sleeve."

VISITATION OF JUDGMENT

Let it be hoped that the present terrible visitation of judgment will be used of God to help bring Germany and the whole world to the Christ of the Bible. Perhaps the case is somewhat different in America, for here, thanks to the propagation by the fathers of Evangelical Christianity, the rank and file of the people have a more intelligent acquaintance with the Bible; consequently, Modernism made slower headway here. Its propaganda has been less bold, more apparently religious, and not as outspoken as it is in certain parts of Europe. Nevertheless, we are traveling in the way of the German Universities of about forty years ago, and are becoming more bold in our defense of the materialistic philosophies. We stop here only long enough to present one of the aspects of this teaching, as seen in our institutions to-day, namely: the oft repeated affirmation that the world, as a result of the operation of the law of evolution, is growing morally better.

A CHARACTERISTIC CONTENTION

This is one of the principal contentions of Modernism. It is far from our purpose to deny the fact of progress as seen in the lives of individuals and institutions, under the influence of Jesus Christ. What should be denied is, the claim that the world at large, independently of Jesus Christ, is growing morally better under the direction of the supposed beneficent law of evolution. As stated, this is one of the most common utterances of the New Theology. Reference is here made to this fact because this is one of their proudest declarations in university and elsewhere, and which has had a direct bearing upon our recent history.

This teaching accounts in no small measure for our recent lack of military preparedness. Advocates of Modernism were opponents of an adequate self-defense. Of course when they saw that war was inevitable, an attitude of silence became expedient; but they did not renounce in any large numbers the false teaching which had almost succeeded in leading the nation into a military debacle. There were some notable exceptions, however, as was illustrated by the case of the late Rev. B. Fay Mills, who had become one of the most ardent advocates of Modernism, but who later publicly admitted his error and renounced its doctrines. Mr. Mills had his contemporary in England in Dr. R. J. Campbell of London.

To this teaching, as advocated in America, a standing army of strength reflected upon the brotherhood of man and the supposed divinity of human nature! Man, they affirmed, is so rapidly advancing in his evolution to a higher type of human brother that a world war was out of the question.

Had it not been for this teaching, not only would we have been prepared many years ago for the most terrible of all wars, but we would doubtless have enlisted to do our part on the side of righteousness at an earlier period in the struggle, if our preparedness would not have prevented this world-wide cataclysm.

Furthermore, had it not been for this teaching well meaning Americans would not have been found participating in the Hague Conferences, to which our greatest prophets never pinned their faith. They know that political peace cannot be assured by moral assent only, that back of moral influence there must be physical force, that civilization at its best has always broken down when the boast of human progress was at its height. But for this sound interpretation of history and Scripture, and also for the lack of confidence in the nature of man, the advocates of the good Old Bible Theology have been referred to as a class belonging to a remote past, notwithstanding the fact that they were the great prophets in America during the world's darkest period in modern history. They were the only ministers of religion that struck the true note.

NEW THEOLOGY REVIVAL

Doubtless, since the war is over, and soon a kind of international peace may have been secured, the advocates of Modernism will re-emphasize the same old deception, and declare that now we see demonstrated the truth of their theory: that man has only been temporarily impeded in his advance in civilization; that he is rapidly growing morally more fit under the beneficent and omnipotent law of evolution—in short, that nothing can defeat him in his upward climb toward the goal of his high destiny. The war put a serious check on this propaganda, though doubtless it will be taken up again with renewed zest.

Of course, they will not tell the world that the new international peace gained is not the result of the teachings of the New Theology, but rather in spite of these teachings. They well know that physical force will endeavor to hold in check the selfish nature of men. Those who know the Truth will not be surprised over the revival of this teaching. Modernism will continue to extol its theories in universities and churches. Let no one be deceived by it. Christ's Church ought to know what is in man—his capabilities, his selfishness, his weaknesses—that there can be no certainty of a permanent discharge in this conflict, so long as man is dominated by the law of self-interest, that these periodic outbursts of brutal aggression will recur, unless the law is sufficiently strong, and men are sufficiently courageous to enforce it. As to the latter, however, time only can tell. Let it be hoped that the law can be enforced; that force will be the master; that its chains will prove sufficiently strong to hold the nature of man in leash.

THE THEOLOGICAL SEMINARY

It is probably true that in no way is the effect of the teaching of Modernism in America more clearly seen than in some of the theological seminaries. Let it be here said, lest an injustice be done to many noble men who are teachers in our divinity schools, that we have only good will toward the theological seminary. The writer owes a debt of gratitude to those majestic souls who, in this institution, gave him of their best. For the churches the seminary has always been one of God's most valuable assets. It is because of the value, the far-reaching influence of this institution that we would see it delivered from the radical criticism of the Bible. But the false teacher has found his way into the seminary. Modernism has, in some cases, almost paralyzed this grand institution.

During the last twenty-five years, the New Theology has succeeded in making the Seminary one of the greatest problems for the churches of Jesus Christ. With the principal denominations, during the past thirty-five years, increasing about one hundred per cent., the divinity schools, in numerous instances, have been at a standstill. At the time of the writer's graduation from the Seminary in 1895, there was an annual attendance of about fifty students, but during the past fifteen years the attendance at this Seminary has averaged about forty, or less. The denominations growing, but, in nearly every case, the Seminaries in the North hardly holding their own. Here then we have a striking illustration of the effect of the radical criticism, the business of manufacturing doubt as to the inspiration and divine authority of the Bible. This alone is the thing that has blighted the Seminary.

And so long as this condition exists no improvement is possible. The New Theology is emptying our churches and our Seminaries, while the Old Theology is filling up the Bible Training Schools. We may hold conferences over the problem of the Seminary but here is our problem, to get rid of every teacher of the New Theology. If this were done and the fact made known to the churches, a new day would brightly dawn for our Seminaries. It would be safe to predict that if these institutions where the destructive criticism is taught should give the management of their affairs for a decade to some of our well known orthodox teachers, we would see these institutions filled with splendid men. But that day of glad revival would be preceded by some radical changes, doubtless by not a few theological funerals. It was a wit who said, "I recommend a certain preacher as chaplain of Sing Sing Prison because he has the faculty of emptying every church where he preached, and I thought he could empty Sing Sing." But that preacher is not needed in some of our Seminaries. The New Theology of pantheistic evolution is doing the work, and no boast of scholarship and love for the Truth can save the situation. Modernism will ultimately empty every religious institution in America where it is taught or turn them into places of secular education.

The author sent free copies of the first edition of his book, *The Modern Conflict Over the Bible* with various pamphlets, to fifteen thousand of our theological students and pastors in various parts of America. This literature called forth numerous letters, nearly all of which were an indorsement of the position taken by the author. The following excerpts from two of the letters received from students in theological seminaries will tell their own story:

DEAR BROTHER:

I have read with much pleasure and profit your new book "The Modern Conflict Over the Bible." I want you to know that we greatly appreciate what you are doing for Evangelical Christianity. You cannot denounce "New Theology" in terms stronger than it deserves. Your book comes to me as a refreshing spring in the desert of theological training, where every cardinal doctrine of Christianity is either questioned or decried. There are yet a few students here who have not been won to the "New Theology" and they deeply appreciate your book.

Very truly yours,

MY DEAR BROTHER:

I am a last-year student in this Seminary. Next May I expect to graduate. When I do graduate I do not know what I shall preach. The blessing of the instruction received here for three years is far from apparent... So irrational has been my instruction that I cannot believe anything just now.

The New Theology has bored me to death, yet I have imbibed enough of its atmosphere of doubt and uncertainty to be assured that I have lost my bearings. Your book hits the nail on the head, and I would like to see some of the "blind leaders of the blind" answer and refute it. I am so tired of the arrogance of the New Theology teacher here, who loses himself in words and is the greatest exponent of word camou-

flage imaginable. I believe he has murdered the faith of
many, whose faith by other methods and more sane ways of
thought and teaching he might have built up. I wish your
book could be put into the hands of every man who is about
to enter an "infected seminary." The New Theology here
has taken away the crutches we had and gave us nothing to
hold us up.

I believe that the new speculation will be the destroyer
of the old faith. I am, sir,

Very truly yours,

The above letters reveal the religious unrest
that exists in not a few of our seminaries in the
Northern States where the New Theology is
taught.

THE COLLEGE AND UNIVERSITY

What is true of not a few of our seminaries
is true also of many of our colleges and universities. In a number of recent issues of *The Sunday School Times,* there was a series of able
articles on the subject: "The Impact of Paganism
in My Own University," in which the writer, a
college graduate, makes plain that our entire university education in the North is shot through
with Prussian rationalism, materialistic evolution, criticism of the Bible, in brief, with the
modern New Theology. These are facts that call
for the most earnest consideration on the part of
the university boards and the churches generally.

We will quote from one of these illuminating
articles:

So I was not greatly surprised, and rather tempted to be amazed were it not so tragic, when our professor explained about Jehovah and other tribal gods of primitive peoples. The book of Jonah was taken as an illustration. The reason that "Jonah rose up to flee to Tarshish from the presence of Jehovah" was because the writer of the book of Jonah regarded Jehovah as a tribal god, who did not have influence in Tarshish. It seemed not to occur to the professor of sociology that the writer of this book of Jonah pictured Jehovah, the tribal God of little despised Israel, as sending his prophet to the mightiest empire on earth, threatening the destruction of that empire in three days unless its people repented of their sin against Jehovah. And at the close of the Book the Bible writer revealed Jehovah as asserting the same rights of personal possession over the people and cattle of Nineveh as he had over Palestine and all the portions of the earth. This was but one illustration of what cropped out again and again in these shallow criticisms of the Bible.

The professor who taught the classes in New Testament Greek, a cultured Doctor of Philosophy, whose ignorance of the Bible was amazing, sat in judgment on religious things and gave the impression that the "orthodox" ideas were relics of a barbarous past. He in common with most of the other professors, believed in being "Christians" and doing good, but the idea that such doctrines as the Resurrection and the Deity of Christ were important, was to him and the others bigotry.

I was to learn, however, that there was something far more dangerous than this superficial criticism of the Bible ·on the part of men who should have confined themselves more closely to the fields in which they were really trained. This, by the way, was one of the curious elements in the religious situation in my university. While each man would defer respectfully to the experts in a different branch of learning, each specialist, whether in English, in Mathematics, or in Language, considered himself perfectly qualified to pass on questions relating to the Bible and Christian faith. The consequence was that they were guilty of historical and scientific errors as grotesque to one who knew the subject as the dramatic criticism of a school-boy would be to a master playwright. Yet these superficial references to the Bible and the ridicule of deep Christian fundamentals passed current with many of the students, and was received by them as of equal authority with opinions in the field in which the professor was qualified to speak.

This lengthy quotation has been given because it is an accurate presentation of the situation in not a few of our higher institutions of learning, revealing the American university to be a menace to Bible Christianity. What college to send our ambitious young men and women to has become a serious question. This is the reward of those noble orthodox Christians who gave of their wealth to make the American college a reality, and source of blessing to the whole world.

STATEMENT OF PRESBYTERY

The statement below was printed in *The Presbyterian* of Philadelphia, Jan. 6th, 1919, one of the representative papers of that Church in America.

PRESBYTERY RESISTING THE UNIVERSITY PAGANISM

The Presbytery of Denver, at its September, 1918, meeting, appointed a committee consisting of Wm. M. Campbell, chairman, Robert T. Caldwell, and J. Mont Davis, to investigate and report concerning the nature of the religious views held and instruction imparted at the Denver University and Iliff School of Theology. These are both institutions of the Methodist Episcopal Church. The purpose of this investigation was to determine whether they were suitable places to which Presbyterian and other evangelical people could safely send their young people for education, but had nothing to do with any attempt at disciplining the institution.

After full investigation, the committee recommended to the presbytery that (a) "Our young people seeking college training be advised to select, if possible, some institution where such pitfalls are neither found or countenanced. (b) That no student for the ministry under our care pursuing his studies at these institutions be recommended to our Board of Education. (c) That in view of the crying need of safeguarding sound doctrine, prayerful and unceasing effort be instituted for the establishment of a college under exclusive Synodical control to meet the worthy needs of the Rocky Mountain region.

Among the teachings which the committee found to be propagated by the teachers and text-books of these schools were these: The theory of evolution is boldly taught as the account of the whole development of man, physically, mentally, and spiritually. All religion, even Christianity, is simply the product of evolution. The account of man's creation as given in Genesis is ignored. All of Genesis up to the call of Abram is legendary. Chronicles was written after the exile, and so was all pertaining to the Levitical Law. There is no such thing as atonement for sin. Each man must bear his own. The deity of Christ is denied. Many other kindred teachings are maintained in these schools.

This Presbytery is to be commended for its fidelity in the exercise of care of the instruction of its young people. Pro-Germanism still lurks in the secret chambers of schools and universities, and it is as deadly and destructive now as it was in the hands of the Kaiser. and his university colleagues. Other Presbyteries, if they be faithful, will need to take like action, and that promptly, for the virus is spreading, like the "flu" or venereal poison. It is no time for indifference or hesitation. Religious and moral quarantine is absolutely necessary. The religious Bolshevists have been so busy and have practiced such German-like subterfuge, shrinking from an open profession of their position, that they have gotten a strong hold upon institutional life and with audacity and atrocity have throttled the religious life in more than one institution.   It is high time that evangelical Christians of all denominations combine to overcome this dire and destructive adversary.   No time should be lost.   We glory in the Denver Presbytery.   More power to them.   May all the others do likewise.

PHILANTHROPY AND THE NEW THEOLOGY

In 1917 the public press quoted one of America's richest and best known citizens—a philanthropist of world-wide note—as saying that he had given $70,000,000 toward the war, including his purchase of Liberty Bonds.

Doubtless this rich man, who is a supporter of Modernism in American education, had not been aware that he was investing his wealth to defeat the New Theology as seen in its harvest of war, suffering and death.   This gentleman has given millions to education.   Could he but fully understand the invasion of his own country by an anti-Christian propaganda, possibly influences would be started that would effect a revolution in not a few of our educational institutions.

If men of material wealth, who have been ensnared by this subtle infidelity, could clearly understand these things, doubtless they would become reservoirs of commanding influence, centers of great moral power in the religious world; they would become the most pronounced Old Theology advocates in America; they would, like true men, come out into the open arena and fight Modernism to a finish; they would be classed as our most valuable citizens, as defenders of the Gospel of Jesus Christ—the old well-tried Gospel, the moral power that alone can stabilize the nation, that has made America great, and in which is found the hope of the world. They would see that the security of the State is to be found only in the grand old doctrines of the word of God.

Thus we have taken a glance at the problem Christian America has to solve. The New Theology has made its contribution to our education and our religious life.

HOW SHALL WE BUILD AMERICA?

We have on our hands a work of separation and extermination of the first magnitude. The smut of a false education has made its mark upon America, political and religious America. And now we must face the task of building a new social and religious order. How this shall be done; what fashion it shall take; what leadership it shall command? The Christian people must furnish the answer, and meet the present challenge and heed the compelling call, as we press forward with God in the upbuilding of the newer society that is emerging from the passing of the older order.

What contribution shall we make? It is evident, as the history of two thousand years abundantly proves, that there is only one Foundation for the upbuilding of a nation, as for an individual, namely: Jesus Christ. But what sort of material shall we employ in building on this only Foundation? Passing through the canyons óf the Rockies the massive rocks showed by their countless layers of strata the various ages through which they had passed. Each deposit was as distinctly marked by the finger of time as if done by an artist's chisel. In these giant rocks, so curiously wrought by nature, so stupendous in power, so suggestive of millenniums of the far distant past, one seems to hear rumblings and groaning, a language such as never before greeted the traveler's ears, and to find in this encyclopedia of knowledge accents of the various chapters of the history of the world. So it is in the history of man. Babylonia, Egypt, Persia, Greece, Rome, Germany, Britain, America, all have made their contribution and history tells the story. What contribution shall America now make?

THE TESTIMONY OF HISTORY

What shall the future historian write of the period upon which we are now entering? Shall ages yet unborn point back with pride and gratitude to the twentieth century and say: "That was the notable period of spiritual and political regeneration, beginning in the year 1914, at the outbreak of the great war, when the liberty loving nations entered into a life and death struggle with a false anti-Bible philosophy and science, and won for all mankind one of the most notable victories of history; when the United States effected a revolution in all its sources of education and knowledge, and entered upon the greatest moral awakening since the dawn of Christianity?'' Or shall the future historian refer to this era as, ''The time of colossal political undertakings, but of social revolutions, and spiritual and national disintegration and chaos, the results of which are seen to this day?''

SHALL THE REPUBLIC BE DISMEMBERED?

It is possible that a few centuries from now there may be no United States of America? Is it possible that, as result of a stupid atheistic education, the giant Republic, like the old Roman Empire, will break up into numerous small warring nations, with as many separate governments as we now have states, comprising within themselves a menace to the world? God prevent it!

It is curious that when a nation becomes recreant to its own high trust how ready it is to cast reflection upon other people, to see the mote in its neighbor's eye but not the beam in its own eye, conscious and boastful of its strength while rapidly pursuing the way of death? Thus we have foolishly acted in adopting the anti-Bible teaching. Yet we flatter ourselves on our security and liberty, while our institutions are reeking with an anti-Christian propaganda, and our social order is infested with anti-Christian elements.

MEN OF THE LUTHER TYPE

We need real Protestants to-day, men of the Luther, Cromwell, Knox, Bunyan, Roger Williams, Wesley type,—the splendid old type who lifted the world to a higher plane of Christian civilization, who stopped at no sacrifice to give us an open Bible, a living, personal, saving Christ and religious liberty. If all this untold treasure were worthy of the sacrifice of the noblest of ages past, surely its preservation is worthy of heroic action on the part of their children. We are justified in making our appeal to young America, to the children of the heroes whose dust is sleeping on the hillsides and in the valleys, to arise like true sons of noble sires and drive from our schools of learning, our churches, libraries and literature, the national and international menace of an apostate religion. The call is being heard to-day. Shall strong brave words be spoken and noble deeds be performed? Shall Protestant America, in the name of the great Master of men, pull down and cast out this intruder? Shall this subtle enemy of the true Faith, who would destroy our Bible, our churches, our happiness, our civilization, who has blighted our world, and whom America, with our brave Allies, have defeated politically on the blood-soaked battle fields of Europe, shall this enemy, in the respectable guise of a false education and religion, be permitted to defeat us at home?

CHAPTER IV

⸙ CONTRIBUTORY CAUSES

BEFORE presenting the most outstanding cause of our present conflict over the Bible, that which has produced the New Theology, we should first state what we mean by the term theology.

THEOLOGY A SCIENCE

Theology is a science, that is, it is a collaborated and orderly system of religious thought setting forth that which men think on such subjects as God, man, sin, Christ, redemption, salvation, etc. The term theology, therefore, may properly be defined as, the science of religion.

TRUE AND FALSE

But there is both a true and a false theology. The true is constructed on the naked teachings of the Bible, the false on philosophy, evolution, science, ethics, speculation, and largely independent of the Bible, using the Bible as an important aid, but not as the one great authority—rather in an accommodating sense. This latter is the New, the former the Old Theology.

THEOLOGY A FASCINATING STUDY

It should be emphasized that theology is the most fascinating, the loftiest, the greatest, by far the most momentous of all studies that can engage the mind of man, for its content has to do with the most far reaching questions covering time and eternity. As someone has said "Every day I live, Politics, which are affairs of Man and Time, interest me less, while Theology, which is an affair of God and Eternity, interests me more." It is important, therefore, that we have a true theology, a science of religion that is built upon the Christian Revelation, for it is evident that everything depends on the views men entertain regarding the great themes which make up the subject matter of theology. For instance, we are told that to hold false views about Christ is to be lost, but to hold correct views as to his nature and work, and to exemplify those in life, is to be saved. (I Cor. 15: 1-3; John 3: 14-18.) How common the remark, "But that is only his theology," as if a man is not as he thinks and acts, or as if thinking has no bearing upon life, conduct and destiny. (Prov. 23:7). The common conception of theology is that it is dry, impractical, worthless, whereas it is the sweetest, liveliest, most inspiring of all studies. Christianity has always flourished under the teaching and preaching of a robust theology. And let it also be stated, with a tremendous emphasis, that when men are not sufficiently interested in Christianity to build a Christian theology then Christianity must languish if not perish.

RELATION OF THEOLOGY TO CHRISTIANITY

It is true that theology is not Christianity, yet it is so vitally, so closely related to Christianity that the latter is largely dependent upon it for its most intelligent and effective expression and propagation. It is amusing to note that those who decry theology all have a little theological system of their own. "Do not preach theology," they say, but religion cannot be taught without using some sort of theology as its vehicle. In a sense Christianity is the soul, theology is the body by which it is expressed; and the soul calls for a sound, healthy, robust body, or theology, that which truly, in terms crystal clear, sets forth the nature, doctrine, and work of God our Father, and the character, purpose or mission of our Lord Jesus Christ.

THEOLOGY AND DOGMA

The objection to theology as a dogma is common and popular to-day, especially among New Theology advocates. But such criticism is amusing were it not the revelation of a deep-seated prejudice, and in many cases of ignorance. Even some teachers in our higher institutions decry dogma. This term is defined by "The Students Standard Dictionary" as "a doctrine," or "as teaching with authority." In the light of this definition Jesus was a dogmatist. Every person of intelligence and conviction is a dogmatist. What is needed is a world of dogmatists who know Jesus Christ personally as Saviour, and who will affirm, declare, or dogmatize about this glorious fact. Christianity is a mighty doctrine, or dogma. It is a life, but for the individual it is a dogma first, for man must first believe a great doctrine concerning Christ before he can enter into this joyous life. Mrs. Mary Baker Eddy decried dogma or doctrine, as do all the New Theology advocates, yet the first step in the study of her system of "mind influence" is to believe one of her dogmas or doctrines, namely; that "all is God and God is all," consequently man is God. And since God is perfect good, man is perfect good.

Since God cannot experience sickness, pain, sin and death, man cannot either, for all these are errors or delusions of mortal mind. *Here is dogma.* And this system teaches that to experience and know God all these doctrines must be believed and mentally practiced. Of course this is Pantheism and a blasphemous falsehood, yet it is "Christian Science" so called, and it is dogma —a doctrine.

THEOLOGY AND FAITH

Even Christian faith cannot become a reality in man until he first hears, listens to the Word of God. And the Word of God is a great doctrine concerning the Father, the Son and the Holy Spirit, and man, sin, and salvation. As the Apostle Paul said: "So then faith cometh by hearing and hearing by the Word of God," (Rom. 10:17). This is rudimentary, for the kindergarten, but it is necessary, to make clear the value of doctrine or dogma in life. Every conviction in life is a kind of dogma, and fundamental Christianity is a doctrine, a dogma, as well as a life.

NEW THEOLOGY FULLY DEFINED

But we must come back and state another word by way of definition as to the New Theology. Of the two hundred and eleven replies which the writer received from as many Presidents of colleges, universities and theological seminaries, in answer to his inquiry as to whether the New Theology, the criticism of the Bible, and evolution are taught in their institutions, and if so whether the students have accepted such teachings as authoritative, it was noticed in many of the replies, the majority stated that they did not know what was meant by the term, New Theology. If it be true that some in our educational institutions do not know what the New Theology is, probably many laymen also are in ignorance as to this teaching.

A definition, therefore, must be here given of the term, New Theology. It is not an easy matter to define this term because the New Theology is the result of a certain mental attitude toward the

Bible in which the Bible is viewed, not as the inspired Word of God, not as the one final authority in the Christian religion, but as of secondary value. We have said that this theology is not built on the Bible, but on ethics, philosophy, evolution, science, and speculation, using the Bible only in an accommodating sense. This should always be kept in mind in thinking of the New Theology.

But it is our duty to submit a definition, notwithstanding the vagueness and speculative character of Modernism. We would therefore submit the following: The New Theology is a false science of religion, or of Christianity, that is built on evolution, rationalism, ethics, speculation, and the results of the radical criticism of the Bible, and that exalts man's reason above Divine Revelation; consequently, this system makes man himself, and not the Bible, the only basis of authority in the Christian Religion. In short, the New Theology means a big superman, and a sort of indefinite, obscure, or impersonal God.

NEW THEOLOGY DESCRIBED

As a more general description of this system it should be said that the New Theology is opposed to all that is commonly known as the Supernatural in religion. There is, in its content, no Supernatural; all is natural, nature; there are no miracles, no supernatural Christ, and no God different in nature from man. All are one. In fact this theology is quite akin to so-called Christian Science and Pantheism. The greatest prophet of this theology is evolution, "the law of evolution," whatever they may mean by that. Jesus is the greatest teacher, but that is all; and He must be interpreted, as must all history, in the light of "the law of evolution." The New Theology therefore is a composite thing—a kind of revival of Unitarianism, of the philosophy of Pantheism, an illustration of evolution in the moral realm, and all abetted by the radical criticism of the Bible, and with sufficient Christian ethics in it to dress it up, and make it appear respectable, as a system of theology.

With the above definition and description in mind we are now ready to advance and see what it is that has led some scholars to adopt this attitude toward the Bible. It has been seen by the definition given that it is a critical and not a submissive or reverent attitude which the speculative theologian has adopted toward the Bible. And this leads direct to the practical query, What are the causes that have produced this critical attitude toward the Bible, and that have resulted in what we call, the New Theology?

PRIDE

Perhaps the first contributing cause we should submit is that element of moral weakness in man's nature, called *pride*—pride of learning, scholarship, intellectual attainments, though it should be

affirmed that this critical school has not a
monopoly on scholarship. For example, how
would Dr. Shailer Matthews, of Chicago University, one of the most boastful of the New Theology
School, compare in scholarship with Dr. James
Orr, the late Dr. Alexander Maclaren, William E.
Gladstone, and numerous others whose names
might be stated? Yet the destructive critics are
continually affirming that all the great scholars
are on their side. They probably mean all the New
Theology scholars who employ the evolutionary
hypothesis.

CHRISTIANITY IS GOD AT WORK

It should not be forgotten that Christianity is
a *Special Revelation* of God which no scholarship
could ever discover. It is a fact that oft'times
the most unlearned know as much about the mysteries of God and His Kingdom as do the most
learned. Scholarship cannot discover God, this
great accomplishment is of the heart, the spirit,
and not of the reason, or intellect. Knowledge
of the sciences will not help here, but knowledge
of Jesus Christ, who reveals the highest Science,
is indispensable. Oft' times learning is a barrier
to the highest knowledge, that is, to a comprehension of the revelation of God in Christ, which
is discovered by experience, for the pride of intellect dislikes to stoop and admit its ignorance
and helplessness in this realm, and become as a
little child (Luke 18:17) at the Master's feet—

the thing which scholarship must ever do if it would enter and learn the mysteries of the Kingdom of Heaven. The great scholar and the poor peasant alike must become as a little child before they can learn the highest knowledge, the science of love, which is the science of God. It would seem that the perpetual boastings of the New Theology school reveal an appalling ignorance of our Lord Jesus Christ and his Gospel; and also constitute a confession on their part that education, culture, scholarship, mental discipline, are the way of salvation, and furnish a password into God's Kingdom, or a key to its mysteries.

DEIFICATION OF MAN

The next contributing cause to the New Theology is an undue *exaltation of the sinful nature of man,* which nature is in opposition to God, is not subject to His holy will, His laws, His love, and of which the Apostle Paul declared, "For I know that in me dwelleth no good thing." (Rom. 7:18). But to this school human nature with all its depravity was, just before the war, divine. Since the outrages committed by this divinity of human nature in Belgium and France, the New Theology advocates are a bit shy of affirming their divinity. Probably after this latest colossal crime is forgotten human nature will again become divine!

Here then is one of the principal causes of our conflict to-day, and of the New Theology, namely:

ignorance of man's nature, his depravity, and consequently the loss of the sense of sin. This is the seed germ from which has grown our modern conflict over the Bible, and we might say, the ever present conflict over the Bible.

The New Theology school would deify that which the Word of God commands us to crucify (Rom. 6:5; Gal. 5:24) and would present to the world a false diagnosis of man, a diagnosis that is contradicted by all the facts of experience.

RATIONALISM

Another cause is found in what is termed, rationalism. The word rational literally signifies reasonable, and is in itself harmless when thus restricted in its meaning. All normal thought is rational.

But this term, as used in philosophy, means reason as opposed to Revelation, or the exaltation of reason as above Revelation and faith. This is what is usually meant by the term, ''The rationalistic philosophies,'' philosophies in which man's reason is supreme.

The rationalist rejects the Supernatural element in the Bible and in life, and exalts reason as above faith, subjecting everything to the analysis of reason; and all that does not appeal to reason, or that cannot be explained by reason is rejected in the religious domain as in every other realm. Rationalism says, the things which are seen and understood are eternal and are to be trusted, but the things which are not seen, as God, Christ, the Holy Spirit, the future state, which are apprehended only by faith, may be superstition and thus may be rejected.

Little time can be given to show the absurdity or unreasonableness of this philosophy, for its fallacy is evident to the most ignorant. For example, because the rationalist cannot explain how sap circulates in a tree, in order to be true to his philosophy he would have to reject this fact as superstition, something above reason, which reason cannot comprehend. Because the rationalist cannot explain the Supernatural and the miraculous element in the Bible; he rejects these as unreasonable, hence untrustworthy, untrue.

CRITICISM OF THE BIBLE

Then again, a certain kind of criticism of the Bible has added much to the modern conflict, and to the creation of the New Theology. It should, however, be stated that there is a proper, a legitimate, a safe and sane criticism of the Bible. "The word 'criticism,' in its original meaning signifies, to judge, or discernment, comprehension." Criticism, therefore, may signify to find fault or to approve, it may be favorable or unfavorable. It is unfortunate that such a term has ever been employed in defining a certain kind of study of the Bible; for to many it is most misleading. But having been adopted we cannot well avoid using it.

There are three kinds of so-called criticism of the Bible.

1. Higher Criticism.
2. Textual Criticism, sometimes called lower criticism.
3. Radical Criticism, called by some destructive criticism.

Taking up the second, or textual criticism, this means the study of the text alone by itself, for the purpose of arriving at its meaning, and is a legitimate "judgment" or "discernment" or criticism of the Bible.

HIGHER CRITICISM

By the term higher criticism, is meant the application of the principles of literary interpretation to the literature of the Bible as we would apply these principles to any other literature, with this exception: We must take into account the spiritual element in the Bible.

In this application an effort is made to ascertain the doctrinal and ethical elements, and the dates and authorships of the various books of the Bible, by a study of the books themselves, of the times in which they were written, and the historical circumstances that would naturally condition thought and expression. Higher criticism when properly used need not be harmful but helpful. Probably most students of the Bible are higher critics, consciously or unconsciously. The human mind naturally inquires, who wrote these books, when were these books written, and what do they teach? In this sense every Sunday-school teacher ought to be a so-called higher critic of the Bible.

It should be stressed, however, that this is only after all a literary study of the Bible, and is far from being the most valuable sort of Bible study. It is related to the Bible somewhat as a scaffold is related to the structure which it surrounds. Unfortunately many of the critics have erected such a conspicuous scaffold, have so magnified this framework that they seem to have lost sight of the great building, or the heart of the Bible, which is the work of God for men. Much valuable time has been wasted in classroom discussing the most non-essential thing about the Bible. When the building is completed the scaffold should come down.

It should also be stressed that the Bible cannot be understood apart from the help of the Spirit of God who gave and inspired this majestic Book. *He alone is the Sovereign Interpreter.* The above critical study is a help, but only the Spirit of God can disclose to the heart and mind of man the treasures of the Bible. *Only He who gave it can correctly interpret it.*

RADICAL CRITICISM

We now come to examine the third, and for our present purpose the most important criticism of the Bible, the radical criticism. As has been seen, a proper higher and textual criticism may be helpful, but this is not the case with the radical criticism of the Bible. Much of that to-day which goes under the name of higher criticism is really radical and unhistorical, destructive, a criticism based on the theory of evolution.

All lovers of God and His Word should be at war against this last named criticism, which has weakened the faith of many, and which has so powerfully aided in the creation of the New Theology.

This kind of criticism has for its method the stating of certain hypotheses, which hypotheses may be reasonable or unreasonable, true or false; usually they are farfetched and unreasonable; and from these they argue to certain conclusions. Let a few examples be submitted in order to illustrate the unscientific and destructive method of this school.

The radical critics are all evolutionists of some sort; consequently, they approach the Bible with their minds already made up as to the method of study to pursue, and as to the character of the content of the Bible.

ILLUSTRATIONS OF RADICALISM

For example: the critic supposes, on the basis of his hypothesis of evolution, that man has been evolved from lower forms of animal life; therefore, to be consistent with his hypothesis he must rule out the account of Creation as given in Genesis, as literal history, and declare that it is poetry, or figurative language, tradition, or a legend, or myth. It matters not how plain the matter-of-fact proof is, as found in Genesis and corroborated elsewhere in the Bible, the book must be twisted and distorted to fit in with the evolutionistic hypothesis. Of course, it *is* readily seen that coming thus to the Bible, with a preconceived opinion, is the unpardonable shame of the critic.

Further, the critic believes that man existed on the earth longer than the Bible is thought by some to teach; therefore, in order to make the Bible fit into, or harmonize with that which the critic believes to be sources of correct information, he would say that Old Testament names as, Adam, Cain, Abel, Enoch, Noah, and others, were not real characters, real men, but names of fictitious persons used to represent dynasties or heads of clans, each covering possibly thousands of years. Thus the critic would harmonize the Bible with his preconceived notion of the age of man on the earth, or in harmony with his hypothesis of evolution, by denying the plainest historical facts recorded in the Bible. It is anything, however absurd, to bolster up the critics' hypothesis as to the period of time man has lived on the earth.

Again, the critic desires to deny the Mosaic authorship of the Pentateuch, and assign its origin to a much later day, probably as late as about 500 or 450 B.C., instead of about 1450 B.C., the time when Moses actually lived and when most of the Pentateuch was written. It should be said that nearly all the critics hold to a much later date for the Pentateuch. Do we ask why? The purpose is obvious, namely:

1.   To make their interpretation of the Pentateuch harmonize with their hypothesis of evolution.

2.   To discredit the evidence from the New Testament as to the miraculous element in the Bible, for Jesus and some other New Testament characters endorsed the Mosaic authorship.

3.   To destroy the doctrine of the Fall and of the redemption of man through blood.

4.   To destroy the trustworthiness of the Pentateuch in order to prove that there was no necessity for God to send His Son into the world to save a lost race; and finally,

5.   To deny by this indirect route, by undermining the historicity of the Pentateuch, faith in the Deity of our Lord Jesus Christ.

It is worthy of note that the critic introduces as evidence against the Mosaic authorship, that which would be considered in any Court of Justice as the most flimsy assumptions. He has no historic proof, he has only a collection of untenable assumptions, and he backs these up by the usual argument, that "the weight of scholarship" is on his side; which of course cannot be true, unless scholarship be defined as, ability to distort facts, and manufacture spurious evidence.

For instance, one of the critics says that to

understand the Pentateuch, we must learn "to read between the lines and discriminate trustworthy from unreliable material." Note, not to discriminate and judge by the text, but by "reading between the lines." Here is what has made such "a heap" of trouble for the critic, and for other people, this sort of unwarranted procedure. We fear the critics are doing more reading "between the lines" than they are reading the lines. It is this reading "between the lines" that has probably led Dr. Charles Foster Kent, Professor at Yale, to prepare a new Bible, made up of what he considered "the parts of our Bible that are probably inspired." At any rate he omitted numerous references to the blood of Christ. Think of interpreting the old Hammurabi Code of Laws, or Blackstone, or even Shakespeare by reading between the lines!

THE CRITICS' CONTENTION

The critics say that Moses could not have written the Pentateuch for the following reasons, among others which we take no time to enumerate. Here we have a sample of their reasoning. They declare that Moses could not have written the Pentateuch and to have received it from God,

1. Because it contains an account of the death and burial of Moses.

2. Because the Pentateuch was written in the third person.

3. Because evidence, they say is at hand, that

the Pentateuch is made up from earlier codes of laws and other sources, and was the result of a growth derived from various documents, covering a period of about one thousand years, or to about 450 B.C., when, they affirm, it was finally edited, or brought together in a body of literature.

It is impossible to fully reply to all the objections to the Mosaic authorship. We shall take time for only a few observations.

MEETING THE CRITICS' OBJECTIONS

The death and burial of Moses are recorded in the last Chapter of Deuteronomy, the final book of the Pentateuch, and stated as a sort of appendix, exactly where we would expect to find it, where it ought to be, as a fitting conclusion to this remarkable history of which Moses was the principal character. This record was put there by Moses' amanuensis, or scribe. Of course this cannot, possibly, be an argument against the Mosaic authorship of the Pentateuch. Moses could not record his own death, and the scribe knew that the history would not be complete without this record.

It was a common custom among the Jews to write or have their writings made in the third person. For example Isaiah in the first chapter verse I, says: "The vision of Isaiah . . . which he saw," etc. The writer has often received letters that were written in the third person, yet written by the first person. It is presumed by some to indicate a mark of distinction or authority. But written by Moses' scribe it was quite fitting as a matter of style that these books should have been written in the third person.

There is no proof that the Pentateuch was made up from laws outside of the nation of Israel or from outside sources. Professor William Frederick Bade, of California, a destructive critic, claims that the Hammurabi Code of laws, written by Hammurabi in Babylon, about 500 years before the time of Moses, furnished material for the Mosaic Code. This is incorrect. The writer took the time to visit the New York Library to study with care this ancient Code, and he found that there is nothing in it that would prove that Moses used any part of it in the make up of his laws. Of course there is a lengthy statement in the former Code as to the punishment inflicted for the loss of an eye or a tooth by assault, but this is not the statement exactly as found in the Mosaic Law. The thing that marks the Hammurabi Code is its striking dissimilarity to the Laws of Moses. As a revelation of justice, and of a high moral standard, there is a comparison between these Codes. The Mosaic is greatly superior to the Pagan Code.

It need not be used as an argument against the Supernatural source of the Pentateuch, the fact that some of the prohibitions found in the Laws of Moses were found in the laws of other nations. Divine Revelation does not contradict common sense. Because theft, lying, murder, and adultery were forbidden in more ancient laws than the Mosaic is not proof that God did not command their prohibition in the laws he gave to Moses. Wellhausen and Kuenen, both destructive critics, rule out the Supernatural. Kuenen in his book on ''Prophecy'' p. 4, says: ''As soon as we derive a separate part of Israel's religious life directly from God, and allow the Supernatural or immediate Revelation to intervene in even one single point, so long our view of the whole continues to be incorrect. It is the supposition of a natural development alone which accounts for all the phenomena.''

This is the position of the destructive critics. God, it is seen, is ruled out. We predict that the days of Driver, Wellhausen, Kuenen, and their like are numbered. The Christian World will never accept them as the ''Ipse dixit.'' The day of extravagant assumptions and hypothesis in the study of the Bible is passing. We must not call these men by harsh names, for Divine Providence and history will assign them to their proper place.

We shall conclude this discussion by submitting the list of reasons given by Profesor George Frederick Wright, D.D., LL.D., of Oberlin, in support of the Mosaic authorship of the Pentateuch.

1. The Mosaic era was a literary epoch in the world's History when such codes of laws were common. It would have been strange if such a leader as Moses had not produced a Code of

Laws. The Tel-el-Amarna tablets and the Code of Hammurabi testify to the literary habits of the times.

2. The Pentateuch so perfectly reflects the condition of Egypt at a period assigned to it that it is difficult to believe that it was a literary product of a later age.

3. Its representation of life in the wilderness is so perfect and so many of its laws are adapted only to that life that it is incredible that literary men a thousand years later should have imagined it.

4. The laws themselves bear indubitable marks of adaptation to the stage of national development to which they are ascribed. It was the study of Naimes' works on ancient law that set Mr. Wiener out upon his reinvestigation of the subject.

5. The little use that is made of the sanctions of a future life, as Bishop Warburton ably argued, evidence an early date and a peculiar Divine effort to guard the Israelites against the contamination of Egyptian ideas upon the subject.

6. The omission of the hen from the list of clean and unclean birds is incredible if these lists were made late in the nation's history after that domestic fowl had been introduced from India.

7. As Rev. A. C. Robinson showed in Vol. VII of the series "The Fundamentals" it is incredible that there should have been no intimation in the Pentateuch of the existence of Jerusalem, or of the use of music in the liturgy or any use of the phrase, "Lord of Hosts," unless the compilation had been completed before the time of David.

8. The subordination of the miraculous elements in the Pentateuch to the critical junctures in the nations' development is such as could be obtained only in general history.

9. The whole representation conforms to the true law of listorical development. Nations do not rise by virtue of inherent resident forces, but through the struggles of great leaders enlightened directly from on high or by contact with others who have already been enlightened.

Dr. Wright adds: The defender of the Mosaic authorship of the Pentateuch has no occasion to quail in the presence of the critics who deny that authorship or discredit that history. He may boldly challenge their scholarship, deny their conclusions, resent their arrogance and hold on to his confidence in the well-authenticated historical evidence which sufficed for those who first accepted it. Those who now are popularizing in Sunday School lessons, periodicals, and volumes of greater or less pretensions, the errors of these critics must answer to their consciences as best they can; but they should be made to feel that they assume a heavy responsibility in putting themselves forward as leaders of the blind when they themselves are not able to see.

The above are words well said by one of America's greatest scholars and religious thinkers.

Thus we have seen by the foregoing facts the principal causes of Modernism, or the New Theology. There is one more cause, however, namely evolution, which should not be overlooked.

EVOLUTION

It is fitting that the question of evolution be considered in connection with Contributing Causes to our modern conflict over the Bible. Probably no philosophy has ever had such an influence over the thinking world as evolution. The acceptance of evolution even as an hypothesis has caused many thinkers to look somewhat askance at the Bible, especially at the account of Creation in Genesis; while others thought they found in evolution sufficient reason for the rejection of the Bible as a final authority on any question in the natural if not in the moral realm. As Haeckel, the German evolutionist said: "With a single stroke Darwin has annihilated the dogma of Creation." And he termed Darwin's Origin of Species "Anti-Genesis."

NEW AND OLD TESTAMENT AND EVOLUTION

But the apparent conflict is not only between evolution and Genesis, it is as real between evolution and the New Testament, as the following quotations will show. "Thou madest him (man) a little lower than the angels, Thou crownedst him with glory and honor, and didst set him over the work of thy hands." (Heb. 2:6-7). "All flesh is not the same flesh; but there is one kind of flesh of men, another flesh of beasts, another of fishes, and another of birds. There are also celestial bodies and bodies terrestrial, and the glory of the celestial is one and the glory of the terrestrial is another." (First Cor. 15:39-40). In Genesis (Chap. 1:27-28) we read: "So God created man in his own image, in the image of God created he him; male and female created he them. And God blessed them and said unto them, Be fruitful and multiply, and replenish the earth, and subdue it; and have dominion over the fish of the sea, and over the fowl of the air, and over every living thing that moveth upon the earth." (Gen. 1:27-28).

It is seen by these scriptures that the New Testament endorses the Old Testament as to the nature, dignity, and glory of man, and his true place in the universe. These quotations show that there is a sharp conflict between the Bible teachings as to man and the theory of evolution—whether it be the theory of materialistic, or theistic, or creative evolution. There is a differentiation here that is impossible to remove—it is eternal.

Notice should be taken of the outstanding facts as taught by the above scriptures.

THE OLD TESTAMENT

Man was made in the image of God. (Gen. 1:27). This is the most remarkable sentence ever written, or revelation ever made known to man, as it places him, in his origin, upon a pinnacle of honor, it reveals man in the day of his sinlessness to be a son of God.

By the image of God is not meant physical likeness, for God is a Spirit, and a spirit has not physical form. A spirit is not physical. The image is in the spirit of man, that is, in his moral faculties, which constitute the real man. What then comprises those faculties, those powers of personality, or a free spirit? They are the powers of thought, feeling, and volition, or the power to think, love, and will. These also are the powers of God, and in a limited way these are the powers of man. Herein then lies the divine image in man, plus the Spirit of God, or the very life of God which communed with man in the day of his innocence. Man was created perfect as we find him in Genesis 1:27. He was endowed with a measure of the Divine Reason.

Evolution, however, teaches the opposite of this. It says that man was made in the image of the lower animal or fish world, and started as a germ or embryo on his long journey of millions of years of growth, through fish and animal, before he became a man in the image of God, as he is to-day. This is the theory of evolution as it relates to man. The evolutionist would say that man was first an imitative animal before he really became a man—a sort of automaton, not a real intelligent human being, but what the evolutionist has termed the "proanthropos" or the missing link between monkey and man.

The New Testament says that there are "various kinds of flesh," and that man is differentiated in his body from all other physical nature. Genesis says that God created every order of life after its kind. Thus here also the New and the Old Testament agree. The former says that man was set over the work of God's hands, the latter that God gave man dominion over all terrestrial creation. Here also the New Testament and Old Testament agree. The New Testament says that man was "crowned" in his creation, "with glory and honor;" the Old Testament says that he was made in the "image" of God. Here also they agree. The implication in the New Testament is that there is no crossing of the species (I Cor., 15:39-40), that each has its own type of life and work to perform. The Old Testament says that each living thing was "made after its kind."

Here also they agree. But in this agreement of Divine Revelation we find, as stated heretofore, the very opposite to naturalistic evolution, or in fact to any theory of evolution. The question naturally arises: Which of these teachings is correct: the Bible or evolution? We have no hesitation in stating that the Bible is correct; that it is the only correct science as to the origin and nature of man.

It is a pleasure to note that scientists themselves are slowly discovering the falsity of their own theories, and the truth of Holy Scripture.

VARIOUS THEORIES OF EVOLUTION

Before proceeding to prove that evolution is passing, that it is unproven, and that its total collapse is probably near at hand, definitions of the various theories of evolution will be given.

1st. There is first the naturalistic or materialistic theory, as expounded by Darwin, and that can be defined as, evolution in physical nature without any God in it. Darwin's theory was, that man is the product of millions of years of growth from various forms of lower physical life.

2nd. There is a popular theory to-day known as, theistic evolution. This may be briefly defined as, evolution with God in it. As to the development of man from lower forms of life, this theory is substantially the same as the Darwinian. It views man as the result of "A continuous chain of causation, a part of which causation is the conscious and purposeful act of the living God, where, in His infinite wisdom and love, there is call for His immediate intervention. This theory holds that behind sequence, and behind age-long development there is an originating and controling Mind, that matter is without meaning apart from spirit." This then is theistic evolution.

3rd. There is a new view which is finding some acceptance here and there—it is the theory of creative evolution. By this is understood, as the term implies, that there is a creative force, or power, or principle, at work in nature, creating continuously, as there is need, and ever moving forward in its unfolding processes and activities, in perfect harmony with the law of its own being, which law is a mystery to man.

This theory of creative evolution seems to be a new name for the old heresy of Pantheism, on which Mrs. Mary Baker Eddy built her theory of Christian Science, and which denies the personality of God. Pantheism says, God is nature and nature is God; both are one and the same.

The writer is not surprised at the appearance of this latest theory of evolution. He predicted twenty odd years ago, in a public address, that evolution was traveling in this direction, and would finally end in Pantheism, and that there it would hold fellowship and communion with its twin sister, Christian Science, so-called. According to this theory, evolution has at last become deified, that is, it is presented as a principle or force in nature, which the Christian Scientists call "good" or God. In short, evolution, according to this latest theory, is God—it has power to create.

DIFFICULTY WITH THE THEISTIC THEORY

Of the three theories the theistic is the most popular in our educational institutions. Those who are unwilling to accept the Revelation of God as given in Genesis and the New Testament have fallen to this theory. First they were Darwinians, but they had to abandon this theory as untenable for Darwinism has been rejected by many noted scientists, though some students still cling to it as a working hypothesis. The theistic evolutionist in the religious world declares that Darwin was wrong but that evolution is true. He is endeavoring to hold on to Genesis as history and also to the Darwinian theory, but under another name, namely, theistic evolution. It is clear that theistic evolution is identical with the naturalistic or Darwinian theory. The only difference is, as stated, the former claims that this is God's method in nature, while the latter makes no such claim. He lays no claim to any special knowledge of God. As to God's method in creation he likes to say, he does not know, hence he disclaims any knowledge of God's method. He rejects Genesis however as authority. Of these two types of thinkers we believe that the Darwinian is the more honest, for to hold to either theory is to reject Genesis; yet the theistic evolutionist inconsistently clings to Genesis. He must stand with Genesis as to the creation of man, or against Genesis and with the evolutionist. There is no middle ground here. It cannot possibly help the believer in theistic evolution to affirm that this is God's method in all life, including the life of man, for evolution is, to this hour, an unproved assumption, while Genesis still stands unshaken!

EVOLUTION DEFINED AND DESCRIBED

What is the theory of evolution that has so powerfully gripped the minds of men, and that has contradicted the record of Creation as given in the Bible?

It should be said that evolution is not simply growth, as seen everywhere in nature, covering the period or generation of every living thing. Nature's process is not an evolution in the sense in which this term is used; it is rather a circle of growth and dissolution, or of birth, growth, decay and death; and dissolution, or death in plants, animals, and human beings are as much a part of the order of nature as is growth, or what is generally but wrongly termed, evolution. Evolution, therefore, cannot be simply growth, for decay and death are as much in evidence everywhere in nature as is growth.

It is difficult to define this theory, even to give the central idea in it, though this we shall try to do. About a dozen different definitions of evolution have been given by able thinkers, some of these by well known theologians. These need not be given here. The following statement will serve to show the central idea in the theory of evolution.

Evolution is a theory (not a law or established fact) which maintains that all life, animate and inanimate, organic and inorganic, is an evolution —that is to say, that all life has developed from a simple or rudimentary form, from the original germ or organism to the homogeneous, and from the homogeneous onward or upward to the heterogeneous, in a series of steps or advances, by which a germ or organism, or the rudimentary part, becomes an adult organism or a fully developed part.

Thus it seems that the theory of evolution is an effort to trace the development of life in all nature, including man, affirming that all visible phenomena and the cosmos are the result of evolution; that these ponderous bodies in space and all life therein or thereon have grown from a single organism of life; that man being a part of this ever evolving order has, like all other antecedent life, come up from a germ and passing on through many millions of years has arrived at what he is to-day. Just how long it has taken man to climb up, the evolutionists differ radically. One writer says, three hundred and six million years; another, thirty million years. Some difference! A long, long human tramp man has had! But when these speculators will have grown more learned and wise in the true science of man, doubtless they will reduce the period of time which man has lived on the earth, and declare with Professor Townsend that there has not been found a trace of human life as having existed on this planet prior to the ice age.

WHAT NOTED AUTHORITIES SAY

Before discussing this interesting question further, it will be well to note what some of the most noted authorities say as to the theory of evolution. We shall quote from an article published in "The Fundamentals," Vol. VIII, by one who called himself "A Layman."

As early as 1889, Professor Virchow, of Berlin, admittedly the ablest anthropologist of modern times, when summing up the results of investigation of this subject by himself and other leading scientists, covering a period of twenty years, declared: "In vain have the links which should bind man to the monkey been sought. The so-called proanthropos, who should exhibit this link has not been found. No really learned man asserts that he has seen him. . . . Perhaps some one may have seen him in a dream, but when awake he will never be able to say that he has approached him. Even the hope of soon discovering him has departed; it is hardly spoken of." Later the same authority declared: "The middle link has not been found and never will be."

Dr. N. S. Shaler of Harvard University; Dr. Etheridge, fossilologist of the British Museum; Professor L. S. Beale, of King's College, London; Professor Fleischmann, of Erlangen, and others give their testimony.

Says Dr. Etheridge: "Nine-tenths of the talk of evolutionists is sheer nonsense, not founded on observation and wholly unsupported by fact. This museum is full of proofs of the utter falsity of their views."

Professor Beale asserts: "There is no evidence that man has descended from, or is, or was, in any way specially related to, any other organism in nature through evolution or by any other process. In support of all naturalistic conjectures concerning man's origin there is not at this time a shadow of scientific evidence."

Professor Fleischmann sums up his estimate of the theory of the descent of man by affirming that, "it has in the realms of nature not a single fact to confirm it. It is not the result of scientific research, but purely the product of the imagination."

Even Professor Haeckel admits in his old age that he, among all his contemporaries, stands alone. "Most modern investigators," he confesses, "have come to the conclusion that the doctrine of evolution and particularly Darwinism is an error and cannot be maintained."

Touching his latest reaffirmation of his naturalistic views, Dr. A. C. Dixon tells us that a scholarly man in Geneva said to him at the time that this statement from Professor Haeckel was "The note of the dying swan," and Haeckel the "Only scientific man of eminence in Germany who believes in Darwinian evolution."

Several notable books bearing on this subject have appeared during the last two years. One by George Paulin, published by Scribners, entitled, "No Struggle for Existence; No Natural Selection," presents an array of facts in support of the two assertions made in this title and against evolution, which must carry conviction to any unprejudiced mind. Another to the same effect is by Professor L. T. Townsend, entitled, "Collapse of Evolution." Still another, and we believe an epoch-marking book, is from the pen of Professor E. Dennert, Ph.D., recently published in Germany, and entitled, "At the Death Bed of Darwinism."

Thus we see that, on the testimony of the great majority of the ablest of its one time leading advocates, the evolutionary theory is in *articulo mortis*. Nay, more, it is already dead, since the spirit (the theory of natural selection) has long since departed. Some of its friends may sit about the remains intently watching for some sign of renewed life, but they watch in vain. And yet there are ministers of the Gospel who, discrediting the Bible narrative of Creation, are still preaching evolution.

The trend of evolution during the past fifty years is to get rid of the Supernatural, the Personal God, to put God out of his world, or to reduce the Deity to a force or principle in nature, dumb and helpless, and thus the result, to show that there can be no special revelation of God as given in the Bible.

GENESIS AND EVOLUTION

What has been stated as to the period of man on the earth is not claimed for the age of the earth. In Gen. Chap. I, verse 1, we read: "In the beginning God created the heavens and the earth." Then there probably follows between the first and second verses a long parenthesis. How long we do not know. Furthermore, what time it took· the Creator to create, or what method He employed in creating the earth, we have no means of determining for a certainty. It may have been by what is called the law of evolution, though of this we are exceedingly skeptical. Genesis states that it took six of God's (creative) days to create this physical universe with all its life. (Gen. 1:3-31). It is profoundly interesting to note that in the science of geology there are what the geologist calls "six geologic days or periods" during which the earth was being developed up to a point when it was fit for human habitation, thus harmonizing perfectly with the record in Genesis; that is, if we interpret the six days in

Genesis as six periods of time which some inter-
preters do.

At the end of the first creative day or period
"the earth was without form or void," (verse 2)
there was incompleteness, a partial chaos, but in
the sixth or last creative day there was not chaos,
but cosmos, a universe of order as it is seen to-day.

This beautiful world having been completed,
God is now ready to crown His creative work by
making man, and giving him this earth in trust,
to use, to have dominion over all its life. In Genesis I, He created matter, in verse 17, He created
animal life, in verse 27, He created man in His
own image. Thus the great creative work was
completed.

Notice closely that it took six creative days or
periods in which to create and fashion the earth
for man's habitation; but it did not take this time,
nor even one of these periods or days in which to
create man, for man was made during some part
of the sixth of these creative days. In other
words, there is not found in this inspired record,
whether the first chapter in Genesis be viewed as
poetry, or figurative, or as literal history, anything to show, or even suggest, that man was or
is an evolution. There is, however, some ground
for holding to the view that the earth was built
up by a slower process, call the method by what
name we may. When science will have discovered
all the facts, if that will ever be possible, the conclusion may be that the earth is the product of

growth, changes, development, but that man has been on this planet, as the Scriptures affirm a far shorter period of time than that assigned by the evolutionist. This is the direction in which science is moving toward a complete vindication of Genesis as the veritable Revelation of God.

CREATION BY DIVINE FIAT

It should also be noted that Creation was by Divine fiat, whatever may be the view as to Genesis. There was a time when God through His Eternal Son created all things by the word of His power. To argue against the fact of Divine fiat is to take the place of an atheist and deny the existence of God and the fact of Creation. Whether God's method in the creation and development of life is or is not the method of evolution, the fact of Divine fiat holds true just the same. Life in all its forms and origins had to have a beginning, had to be created. To argue against Divine fiat is to say that there can be an effect without an adequate cause, a creation without a Creator. Creation is not evolution.

SCIENCE CONFIRMS GENESIS

The fact is worthy of special notice that science has confirmed Genesis, by making clear that evolution cannot create new genus. God created each genus ''after its kind.'' A potato may become many varieties of potato but never a pumpkin. A pair of pigeons may grow into many varieties of pigeon but never into a chicken. Animal did not develop into man, nor will man develop into any higher order of being. This is Genesis, and this is confirmed by the best science.

We will conclude this chapter by making some

GENERAL OBSERVATIONS

1. What has been stated does not deny the fact of a moral or spiritual growth, as seen under the creating, transforming, and unfolding power of God. Happily not a few know much of this "new creation" and development, for we have felt its power, seen it manifest in the lives of others, studied it at close range, saw it unfold, ennoble, and beautify the penitent and obedient life, up to the very last moment at death. And even then it seemed that we could almost discern the presence of the heavenly attendant waiting for the redeemed child, as the latter smiled farewell, and closed the natural vision on loved ones and earth scenes for a time, and then moved on with the heavenly escort to the glorious home in the Father's house. This kind of evolution (if we are justified in so describing it?) which begins in spiritual regeneration, or in what our Lord called the second birth, or the birth from above, is manifest in every generation. Between the Bible and this transformation from the natural to the spiritual there is the same harmony as between the fragrant rose and the seed from which

it sprung, or between the warm, cheering, lifegiving ray of light and the majestic sun that loaned it to this frozen world in order to make it a fitting place for human habitation. This kind of evolution, or, better, transformation, is worth knowing, which results from the new birth of man under the influence of the Gospel and Spirit of God, and which our educators should spend more time in teaching, instead of laboring to prove the unprovable, or to discover what never can be discovered, namely: that man is the result of an evolution from the lower animal world.

2. There have been many theories of evolution put upon the market, and it is astonishing how quickly these have been accepted by superficial thinkers, by those who are looking for some theory that will appear as a justifiable excuse from acknowledging the Bible as the Word of God. It seems to-day that, notwithstanding the fact that Darwinian evolution has long since been abandoned by the greatest authorities on this question, not a few of our teachers still persist in teaching it. In fact every poorly informed student in our schools and out, seems to feel that he must announce himself as an evolutionist in order to be thought of as "learned" and "up-to-date." Even the president of one of the schools of New Theology, in a recent communication to the writer, said, in speaking of religious problems, "that evolution, New Theology and higher criticism," by which last statement is meant the

radical criticism, "have become a part of our ordinary thinking, like the law of gravitation." Perhaps it is popular to indulge in such a statement so near the great center of "German Kultur" in New England, from which institution it is generally understood that seldom one graduates who is not more or less a convert to Unitarianism or the New Theology.

Why is it that to this day not a few undergraduates and graduates, young preachers and school teachers, doctors and others, half educated folks in all the professions affirm that evolution is an established fact? Even many of these are believers in naturalistic evolution, the Darwinian theory, though the latter has long since been given up as untenable. Darwinian evolution, as already stated, is nearly dead. Yet students joke about our ancestors as "living in trees and as tadpoles and fish," and are more dogmatic about it than Darwin ever was.

3. The theory of Darwinian evolution persists even yet as an hypothesis. The teacher in science and the "prep" alike must "boost" the unproved hypothesis. In biology, psychology, archæology, and in some quarters even in theology evolution is still the working hypothesis. But this would not be so objectionable if the teacher did not teach it as an established fact—this "jungle" of unproved assumptions. Possibly if the teacher should get out of the old rut, "the

hypothesis of dirt" as it has been called, and show originality and independence of thought, he would be viewed as "unscholarly," "unscientific," "behind the times;" and, if in New England, he might not experience a rapid promotion. From all this we must conclude that the time has come for some "unlearned," "ignorant," "bold fellow," as the chief Pharisees love to call our most intelligent students, to "bust" this cheap thing, to prick this bubble of an "established evolution."

LAITY IN IGNORANCE

Thus we have seen the principal contributory causes of the New Theology. The vast bulk of the laity are not aware of the fact that the foregoing furnish us with a true explanation of the vast religious unrest, the disintegration and falling away from the churches, and constitute the modern conflict over the Bible. But this no well informed person can deny. There are those who refuse to accept these facts, who endeavor to show that the New Theology has not had its rise in the philosophy of evolution, of rationalism, the destructive criticism of the Bible, and in the nature of man. It is clear, however, that all such view the Bible, not as the one great authority in the Christian Religion, but as furnishing illustrations in history of the development or out-working of the law of evolution in the moral or spiritual life of man. Where the Bible and evolution come in conflict those parts of the Sacred Word are brushed aside as irrelevant, or are viewed as legendary, or traditional, or are given a false interpretation.

CHAPTER V

THE CONFLICT AND ITS PROBLEM

PERHAPS to many thoughtful persons, living the life of quiet simple faith, it may seem strange that there should be a conflict over so good a book as the Bible, the doctrines of which are holy, precepts binding, histories true. Nevertheless such is the fact; a great struggle is on in America—more in evidence than in any period of our history. This conflict has been forced upon us by the school of critics, by that class of men who are battling against the very existence of the Evangelical Churches of Jesus Christ.

With few noble exceptions, here and there, men in both pulpit and pew have closed their eyes to our religious peril. Indeed, in the silence of the orthodox pulpit is found one of the most serious aspects of the situation. If the clergy had only spoken out and informed the people the churches would be fully competent to deal with the problem, without the need of any outside help from such books as this. But the rank and file are kept in comparative ignorance of the growing menace to the cause of Jesus Christ. Many of the Shepherds are not wisely protecting and instructing the sheep. Our flanks are exposed everywhere. Not a few of the churches are very much like an army whose scouts and officers are having some secret dealings with the enemy, while at the same time the latter are attacking on every hand. It would seem that some of the "prominent members" in certain localities are being bribed to inaction by a cunning intriguing policy on the part of certain financial powers. Even in our great training camps where our young officers receive their equipment for battle, spies have become entrenched and are busy destroying the morale of the army of the Lord.

There should be small room for the indifferent when the churches ought to be engaged in one of the most momentous struggles in history for the God-given right to preach and defend the Gospel of Jesus. God is calling His people to-day with a mighty call. It is a call to the open arena, to the battlefields of spiritual conflict, for each to do his part, under the guidance of the Holy Spirit, in the very light of God.

That there is a conflict over the Bible, should be evident to the most careless observer in the churches; nevertheless, many persons are not quite certain as to what this general unrest is all about. Of course it is rather indefinite to say that it is over the Bible. What is there in the Bible to which Modernism objects?

To be specific it should be stated that the following statements cover the ground completely, though not all of these will receive attention in this volume.

THE CRUX OF THE BATTLE

1. The trustworthiness of the Old Testament as history.

2. The Supernatural element in the Bible.

3. The miraculous element in the Bible.

4. The inspiration of the Bible.

5. The doctrines of the Bible.

6. The authority and infallibility of the Bible.

7. The method of interpretation of the Bible.

8. The eternal Sonship and Deity of our Lord Jesus Christ.

9. The Incarnation of the Son of God in flesh.

10. The atonement of Jesus Christ for sin and guilt.

11. The Resurrection of Jesus Christ.

12. The Personal Coming of Jesus Christ.

13. The purpose, authority, and ordinances of the Gospel.

14. The official inauguration and governmental manifestation of the Kingdom of God on earth.

15. The Resurrection of the body in likeness to Christ's Body.

16. The fact of Hell, and the result of sin as seen in the loss of the soul.

17. The fact of the Fall of man and the need of a Divine Saviour.

18. The personality of Satan.

It is seen that the above covers the whole Bible,

and that in this conflict the very existence of the Christian Church is at stake, that is, as an evangelical and Divinely-appointed soul-winning institution.

THE TRUE CHURCH WILL TRIUMPH

Let it be here stated with a *tremendous emphasis* that we have no concern as to the ultimate triumph of the Church. Our concern, rather, is for the teaching, the ministry or service of the Church in the world to-day, for the lost and perishing that are dependent upon the Church for salvation, and for the sheep that have no true shepherds. The Bible will live; but we are concerned that it shall not be emasculated and prevented from having untrammeled expression. The critics may succeed in luring men and women away from the Bible as the voice and comfort of God to human hearts, but they can no more destroy the Bible as a Divine Revelation than they could banish the stars or break up the rock-ribbed framework of our planet. What we demand is that these men shall be prevented from occupying prominent positions wherein they carry on their work of destroying the faith of men in the Bible as the Word of God. We demand that the Sacred Word shall be permitted to do its own appointed work. The New Theology teachers have tried to chain up and strangle the Bible, or to make it speak, if at all, in an unknown tongue; but we insist that they shall set the Bible free, that the Christian people shall put an end to the array of insidious falsehoods in modern teaching that have been launched against the inspiration of the Bible. The time has come when these men should be prevented from masquerading around under the guise of a pretended scholarship and the cloak of religion. There is something far more important than that the critics should draw generous salaries from funds furnished by orthodox believers in the Bible as the Word of God; and that *something is the faith of two million students* who comprise the flower and hope of American Christianity. We demand that the false teacher of Modernism shall be unfrocked. And listen my friend: If God spares the writer he fully expects to see the day when a New Theology teacher will not be found occupying a chair in any evangelical institution throughout this broad land, for the hour of his exit is at hand!

THE BIBLE AND SCIENCE

Ours is not a conflict between science and the Bible, for true science is the hand-maid of Christianity. As Lord Kelvin, that prince of scientists said, "If you think strongly enough you will be forced by science to the belief in God," and he could well have added, to the belief in Jesus Christ, for Christianity is the most self-evident, the greatest of all the sciences; and it does not require a college degree to demonstrate that fact.

Science being classified facts, systematized knowledge, generally in the realm of law, how can Christianity have any fear therefrom, or come into conflict therewith? Christianity must ever be the true friend of demonstrated facts.

SPECULATION IS NOT SCIENCE

Much, however, that goes under the name of science is mere assumption, speculation, fine spun and unproven theories. Of course we are aware that a science can be built out of falsehood, so far as the formulation of the system is concerned. We have a striking illustration of this in that which the school of destructive critics call, "the science of historical criticism." It should be called the science of guessing, for here is where it is seen at its worst, as applied to the study of the literature of the Bible.

CHRISTIANITY WELCOMES INVESTIGATION

But Christianity has nothing to fear from science, for it works in the clear light of day, welcomes investigation and seeks for proof. One of its great declarations is: "But he that doeth truth cometh to the light that his works may be made manifest that they are wrought in God." (John 3:21). Christianity is for the ripest scholarship, the strongest intellect, for all those who desire to investigate and learn the facts of the universe, as it is also for the most humble and ignorant. The controversy that Christ has with men is, that they will not investigate His claims and put Him to the test, that is, demonstrate Him scientifically in the realm of human experience. Christianity is not a pleasant companion for him who fears to investigate, nor for the fakir, for it is a bold, masculine religion, and never on the defensive. Men seem to know this; hence only the open, frank, honest souls are fearless of Christianity and ever ready to prove its claims. Jesus Christ was most explicit on this matter. He knew that His Truth could be demonstrated and as such only can it be known. Christianity is a fact, but it is more, it is a life, and science cannot be in opposition to fact and life.

CHRISTIANITY AND RELIGION

But while this is true of Christianity and science, yet it may not be true of Christianity and religion. A clear distinction should be made between Christianity and religion, for the latter may mean anything. How many the crimes that have been committed in the name of religion! Religion is too loose, too general and indefinite a term, susceptible of many definitions, while Christianity is practical, specific, concrete, intelligible and never abstract in its relation to men.

DID JESUS HAVE RELIGION?

Did Jesus have religion? Verily, if we define religion as dependence or reliance upon God. But religion may mean a great variety of things. It may consist of superstition and prejudice, or merely outward ritual, or form, or any kind of vague, strange notions, the creation of the imagination, trust in dogma, as the infallibility of the Pope, etc., or anything not revealed in the Word of God. But there was a sense in which Jesus was not religious, that is, as the term was understood in His day. Outward formalities had no place in the religion of Jesus Christ only as they set forth a great reality. He would not have established the great symbols of baptism and the supper in His Church were it not for the fact that these outward forms represent the central and fundamental realities of His own work for men. But Jesus had little patience with a mere display of outward forms or, of what someone has called "ecclesiastical millinery." And it was because of this, His attitude toward the religion of His day, that the priests viewed Him as one having no religion, and sought to put Him away by death.

WHAT SHALL WE DO WITH RELIGION?

But should this lead us to say, away with the term religion? Yes, if it supersedes in popular usage the far richer term, Christianity. It were better to hear more of the latter and less of the evasive, vague, though popular term, religion. The term religion is more acceptable with those who desire to be indefinite, "broad-minded," and to avoid such personal endearing terms as "Our Father," "The Lord Jesus Christ," etc. If defined in the light of Christianity then the term religion may properly be used in dealing with Christian Truth.

CLEAR DISTINCTIONS NECESSARY

We have said all this because we want to make a distinction between Christianity and the loose term, "religion," for the former is more meaningful than the latter. Christianity is in essence kindness, sympathy, love, helpful service for men under the leadership of Jesus Christ, and true devotion to and worship of God as Father as He has revealed Himself in His Son. Therefore, between Christianity, a great historical and experimental fact, centering in a living person—Jesus Christ—and science, there can never be a conflict. The strife to-day is between Christianity on the one hand, and a false system of science on the other hand, a something that goes under the name of science, but that is only speculation and wholly undemonstrated as fact. The conclusions of the so-called school of scientific, historical criticism of the Bible, furnish us with numerous illustrations of this, as do many of the text-books used in the schools to-day on such subjects as biology, archæology, psychology, and theology.

THE BIBLE AND GEOLOGY

Not a few persons have declared that there is a conflict between the Bible and the science of geology, and that the Bible is not a text-book on science, though it is the world's greatest text-book on science. Genesis, for example, gives the only truly great revelation of the fact of Creation. It makes plain what we need most to know about the origin of man and the universe, to wit: that they are the result of Divine purpose and fiat, the product of an intelligent Personal Creator. The Book of Genesis, for example, is the greatest authority on geology. All other productions are only illustrations to make clear the facts of Genesis. All the facts of geology agree with Genesis. Mr. James B. Tannerhill, a thoughtful layman of Granville, Ohio, in his book, "Naamah and Nimrod," says, on page 221, in speaking of Genesis:

How wonderful that a writer more than three thousand years before anyone had ever dreamed of what geology would teach, could give such a vivid description of God's steps in fitting the earth for man's habitation. If the Bible could give no better proof of Divine inspiration than the first chapter of Genesis, it is enough!

And Mr. Tannerhill adds:

The description given by Moses of the geological changes the earth went through, and the appearance of life in geologic periods is the most wonderful thing in all literature either sacred or profane.

And again:

Let the man who says that Genesis does not agree with science go hide himself. He is too small and ignorant to be called a man.

This last statement is an hyperbole, but **Mr. Tannerhill** has stated a fact as to Genesis.

God has spoken to man in nature, for the heavens and the earth reveal His glory. The God of Revelation is the God of nature, and nature and revelation are not contradictory, one of the other. Genesis is a revelation, and descriptive of God's method in Creation. We can heartily endorse the words of the late Sir Robert Anderson: "Scientific faith compels belief in God." Genesis is the only text-book on Creation; and it is the greatest authority on geology. There is **no** conflict between the Bible and true science.

THE BIBLE AND PHILOSOPHY

There need be no conflict between the Bible and philosophy, that is, so long as philosophy knows its place and keeps within its proper bounds. The philosophy of a thing is the rational explanation of that thing, so far as an explanation can be given within human limitations, as to why that thing should be.

Philosophy concerns itself little with origins or causes of life, it confines itself to visible phenomena, claiming that we can know only what appears to the senses or in feeling, and nothing of things as they are in themselves, or of causes. Philosophy, therefore, is a proper study.

PHILOSOPHY GENERALLY SPECULATIVE

It should be stated that philosophy is generally speculative in character, and cannot be considered as on an equality with the Word of God. This fact makes it clear that philosophy need not come into conflict with revealed Truth, unless its hypotheses contradict the teachings and authority of the Bible. For instance, the philosophy of evolution is viewed by some as an established fact in the moral and spiritual life of man, for here they claim that they observe a continuous development, an upward ascent of man from the lower to the higher in the new spiritual life in Christ. If Christian growth can be called evolution, then the Apostle Paul gave us a true formula when he said: "But we all with open face beholding as in a glass the glory of the Lord are changed into the same image from *glory to glory* even as by the Spirit of the Lord." (II Cor. 3:18). If this be evolution, then it is the only established evolution, all other theories of evolution are unproved hypotheses, though we doubt the wisdom of referring to moral growth as evolution. Between this view of moral evolution, however, and the Bible there can be no conflict.

THE BIBLE AND THEOLOGY

There is also no conflict between the Bible and true theology, for true theology is an unchanging, systematized body of truth.

If theology were "a progressive science," as is the claim of Modernism, then there would be a conflict between it and the Bible, for what is changing in its content cannot be a true science. For instance, what was true yesterday, in the realm of man's relation to God and God's relation to man, cannot be false to-day, and vice versa. They tell us that "each generation must make its own New Theology." But true Christian theology is a systematized presentation of the teachings of the Bible, using for its facts or data the Bible only, and is the Bible constantly undergoing change? There is some truth that may be found outside the Bible, but all revealed Truth, the Truth·which makes up our systematic or Biblical theology, is found exclusively within the Bible. It is untrue and harmful to make any distinction between systematic and Biblical theology, for in so doing the admission is granted that there can be a Christian theology built outside of the only source of information—the Bible.

IS TRUTH EVER CHANGING?

To admit that theology is a progressive, ever-changing science, is to admit that Truth is ever-changing. But Truth never changes; it is only our understanding of Truth that may change. But the New Theology school is forced to this dilemma, because it claims that the Bible is not our only source of, or foundation for theology. They would include modern science and philosophy as sources also, equally with the Bible. But science and philosophy are undergoing constant

change. Much that was taught as true yesterday
in these studies is viewed as false to-day. Consequently, the rationalists must call their theology
''a progressive science'' in order to keep company,
(not with the Bible, with the Truth which never
changes) with philosophy and science that are
constantly undergoing change. We repeat, there
must be a conflict between the Bible and theology
if we admit the contention of the New Theology.
And this is exactly what we find in Modernism.
It is at war with the Bible, for it has broken away
from ''the Book'' as the one and only true foundation for a Christian theology. Individual Christian experience cannot be a safe guide here for
the experience of each individual differs in part
from every other individual's experience.

OLD THEOLOGY IS STABLE AND SURE

The Old Theology is stable and sure. It is not
changing or fluctuating, for it builds on the Bible
only. If the Bible were subject to change from
generation to generation, if Revelation were a continuous, progressive, ever-enlarging reality, then,
of course, each generation must get its own
revelation and build its own theology. But such
is not the case. The only Revelation men receive
to-day is an illumination of mind and heart to
understand what God has already revealed in His
Word, and this is illumination rather than revelation. It is true men may make a more perfect or
a less perfect interpretation of the Bible to-day

than they did yesterday, and to this extent alone can their theology be modified or changed in any particular. But this is so seldom done that it need not make any difference in the character of Christian doctrine from generation to generation. Men want to feel and know that the theology or doctrines of the Apostolic Church, for example, are the doctrines or theology of the Church to-day. We do not want an ever-changing Christ, nor a changing Christian theology. Here the human mind seeks for stability and unchangeableness. Faith demands this. It wants to know that that which was true for past centuries is true for us to-day; that God's unchanging Truth for the first century is God's unchanging Truth for the twentieth and for all centuries, though it may be formulated in a somewhat different terminology; and that it does not need to be doctored up in order to make it harmonize with the latest postulates of science and philosophy. ،

NEW THEOLOGY AN IMPOSSIBILITY

To say, therefore, that a theology is best and truest because it is new, and that the Old Theology must needs be false because it is old; that what was true for those of a far gone past may be false for us to-day; that each generation must manufacture its own theology is to reveal stupidity that is amazing, and to make clear why we have a conflict over the Bible. They say the Old

Theology was true for the long ago but it is not true for us to-day; but they do not tell just where it ceased to be true, in what year or period of the Christian era.

Let it not be imagined that these men are idiots, for many of these new theologians are scholars, and some of them worshippers of "scholarship," and, mark you, "modern scholarship" at that; that is, the scholarship that presents Modernism as their only point of view. This then is their learned contention. We have heard them teach it and preach it. "Theology is an ever-changing and progressive science." Whose theology? Not that revealed from heaven! Man's theology, that which is built on the shifting sands of human knowledge.

ANOTHER NEW THEOLOGY DILEMMA

It is probably true that this explains another point of view of Modernism, namely, that the theology that would be true and helpful for the Chinese or natives of the Fiji Islands may not be true and helpful for the more highly educated peoples. This claim implies a double standard of morality and religion for different races and grades of intelligence. But God knows no double standard. His Gospel has a universal application to all men alike, and has an Infinite power of adaptation as it meets every changing condition and circumstance in life.

TRUTH CANNOT BE LABELED NEW

It is clear from what has been stated that the true theology is neither new nor old, that being a scientific formulation of Revealed Truth it cannot come into conflict with the Bible, that God's Truth is always new and up-to-date, and far in advance of men, that only the ignorant condemn a theology because it is old, and embrace a teaching because it is labeled as new, "up-to-date."

THE ONLY TRUE TEST FOR THEOLOGY

Here is the test for any Christian theology: Does it present Jesus Christ as Very God of very God, and the Father in Him making a complete provision for the putting away of sin, reconciling through His blood the world unto Himself? This is the never-changing Old Theology of the Bible —that has the mark of blood upon it, that sees the open grave, that declares an eternal salvation, a new life, a regenerated earth and race, a returning Lord and King, and a perfect civilization as the result of the final triumph here of the glorious Kingdom of God.

It has already been shown that our conflict is real, that there is a differentiation between the so-called New and the Old Theology that is eternal, that the difference is not, as they say, "one of emphasis only," and that this conflict will continue until this false system of denials as to the Bible, is swept away. When the New Theology school will learn to take the Bible, as to its purpose and history, for what it is and so teach it, then and not till then will the conflict cease.

INFIDELITY AND CRITICISM

It is interesting to note, that the pioneer European and American critics of the Bible have pursued very much the same method of literary criticism as that followed by Thomas Paine in his "Age of Reason;" consequently, we need not be surprised at knowing that both have, in many cases, arrived at the same conclusions. The school of the destructive critics, which has become so dominant in many parts of our higher education, received much of its inspiration from agnosticism and infidelity. The critics have lighted their little lamps from the dim flickering light of infidelity.

THE SAME METHOD

It is also interesting to note that the modern critics have pursued the same method as outlined by infidelity in its attacks on the Bible; they both have traveled the same road. Their first attack has invariably been on Genesis, their last on Jesus. One of Ingersoll's early lectures was entitled: "The Mistakes of Moses." It was only in the latter years of his life that he launched his assault on the character and mission of our Lord. Thus Paine began his criticism of the Bible, and thus he ended. A wit, in commenting on Ingersoll's lecture, said: "It is easy to criticise a dead man. If Moses were alive it would be interesting to hear him lecture on "The Mistakes of Inger-soll." And so it would.

METHOD IN THEIR MADNESS

It will be seen that there is method in their madness. The strategy of Satan is worthy of close study. By their method the critics reveal a shrewdness and cunning that illustrate the truth of the words of Jesus, when He said: "The children of this world are in their generation wiser than the children of light" (Luke 16:8). Right well they know that Genesis with its promised Messiah is the key to the Bible. If the destructive critic can undermine Genesis the whole structure will collapse; consequently, the almost superhuman efforts these critics of the Word of God have been making in recent years to discredit Genesis, and the Pentateuch generally, denying the Mosaic authorship, putting the date of its final composition as late as 450 B.C., describing Genesis as made up of "tradition," "poetry," "myth," "figurative language," and not a real trustworthy record of Creation, and of the times of which it speaks. First, the critics said that the Pentateuch was a product of the time of David, or probably about 850 B.C. Later they brought the date down to 700 B.C., then 600 B.C., then 500 B.C., and now the latest date they have assigned is 450 B.C. We need not be surprised if the next assignment will be 299 B.C., and with it the sensational announce-ment that in a deep cave in Mount Lebanon was found, by the distinguished scholar and archæologist, Dr. Rabbi Wisemann, the bones of Jesus Christ, together with a manuscript containing an account of His resuscitation after His Crucifixion and burial in Joseph's tomb.

BUT WHY EMPHASIZE GENESIS?

In Genesis we have the foundation and beginning of everything. For instance, Genesis tells us that God created the heavens and the earth. The vital interest and relation of religion to Genesis are explained by Professor James Orr, one of the most noted Bible scholars of our day, as explained in Vol. VI. p. 80-86, "The Fundamentals." He said:

The interest of religion in the record of Creation is that this doctrine is our guarantee for the dependence of all things on God, the ground of our assurance that everything in nature and Providence is at His disposal. "My help cometh from the Lord which made heaven and earth."

And Professor Orr adds:

Suppose there were anything in the universe that was not created by God—that existed independently of Him—how could we be sure that that element might not thwart, defeat, destroy the fulfilment of God's purposes? The Biblical doctrine of Creation forever excludes that supposition.

In the first chapter of Genesis we have an account of Creation. In the second and third chapters we have a description of Creation and the record of the Fall of man. There are not two

narratives here, as the critics affirm, one contradictory of the other. The second and third
chapters relate to God's dealings with man and
man's transgression. In fact, the Fall of man
furnished us the key to all that follows in the
Bible by way of Divine Purpose. The whole story
of the Bible is of a world turned aside from God,
disobedient, resisting His grace. As Professor
Orr said:

If the story of the Fall were not at the beginning in Genesis,
we would require to put it there for ourselves in order to explain
the moral state of the world as the Bible pictures it to us, and
as we know it to be. . . . The story of the Fall is not a myth
but enshrines the shuddering memory of an actual moral
catastrophe in the beginning of our race, which brought death
into the world and all our woe.

GENESIS STANDS UNSHAKEN

The destructive critics have tried to break down
Genesis but have hopelessly failed. They have
said that the Creation story was a Babylonian
myth, but the scholars know that this is not true.
As Professor Orr has further said:

The old Babylonian creation myth is a debased, polytheistic,
long-drawn out, mythical affair, without order, only here and
there suggesting analogies to the divine work in Genesis. The
old flood story of Babylonia has much more resemblance, but
it also is debased and mythical and lacks wholly in the higher
ideas which gives its character in the Biblical account. Yet
this is the quarry from which the critic would have us derive
the narratives in the Bible. They say the Israelites borrowed
them and made them the vehicles of nobler teaching. . . .

There is not only no proof that these stories were borrowed in their crude form from the Babylonians but the contrast in spirit and character between the Babylonians' products and the Bible's seem to me to forbid any such derivation. The debased form may arise from corruption of the higher but not vice versa. Much rather may we hold with scholars like Delitzsch and Kittel that the relation is one of cognateness, not of derivation. The Genesis traditions came down from a much older source and are preserved by the Hebrews in their purer form. This appears to explain the phenomena as no other theory of derivation can do, and it is in accordance with the Bible's own representation of the line of revelation from the beginning along which the sacred tradition can be transmitted.

GENESIS AND SCIENCE

It may be well to give here a summary of the reasons as given by Professor Orr why Genesis is an agreement with the best science. There is:

(1) The truth that man is the "last of God's created works—the crown and summit of God's creation."

(2) There is the great truth of the unity of the human race. No ancient people that I know of believed in such unity of the race, and even science until recently cast doubt upon it. How strange to find this great truth of the unity of mankind confirmed in the pages of the Bible from the very beginning. This truths holds in it already the doctrine of monotheism, for if God is the Creator of the beings from whom the whole race sprang, He is the God of the whole race that sprang from them.

(3) There is the declaration that man was made in the image of God—that God breathed into man a spirit akin to His own—does the science of man's nature contradict that, or does it not rather show that in his personal, spiritual nature man stands alone as bearing the image of God on earth, and

founds a new Kingdom in the world which can only be carried
back in its origin to the Divine creative cause.

(4) I might cite even the region of man's origin, for I think
science increasingly points to this very region of Babylon as
the seat of man's origin. Is it then the picture of the condition in which man was created, pure and unfallen, and the
idea that man, when introduced into the world, was not left
as an orphaned being—the divine care was about him—that
God spake with him and made known His will to him in such
forms as he was able to apprehend—is it this that is in contradiction with history? It lies outside the sphere of science
to contradict this. Personally I do not know of any worthier
conception than that which supposes God to have placed
Himself in communication with man in living relations with
His moral creatures, from the very first. Certainly there would
be contradiction if Darwin's theory had its way, and we had
to conceive of man as a slow, gradual ascent from the bestial
stage, but I am convinced, and have elsewhere sought to show,
that genuine science teaches no such doctrine. Evolution is
not to be identified off-hand with Darwinism. Later evolutionary
theory may be described as a revolt against Darwinism, and
leaves the story open to a conception of man quite in harmony
with that of the Bible.

On the question of the patriarchal longevity, I would only
say that there is here on the one hand the question of interpretation. . . . But I would add that I am not disposed to
question the tradition of the extraordinary longevity of those
olden times. Death, as I understand it, is not a necessary
part of man's lot at all. Had man not sinned he would never
have died. Death—the separation of soul and body, the two
integral parts of man's nature—is something for him abnormal,
unnatural. It is not strange then that in the earliest period life
should have been much longer than it became afterwards. Even
a physiologist like Weismann tells us that the problem of science
to-day is that—not why organisms live so long, but why they
ever die.

JESUS AND GENESIS

It is clear from the above facts as stated by one of the most renowned scholars of our time, that Genesis is fundamental as history and Revelation. It is not an exaggeration to say that if the trustworthiness of the Pentateuch were destroyed, Christianity would no longer hold the field as a Supernatural Revelation. Time does not permit of details here, but this is, as stated, a vital matter. Genesis is the historical foundation and background. Jesus Christ is the keystone in the arch. Jesus affirms that Moses wrote of him, the destructive critics say that Moses did not write of him. (John 5:46; Mark 10:5; Luke 20:28). But we shall stand by Genesis as we do by Jesus for both reveal the power, wisdom and love of the Triune God. Genesis gives us a scientific statement as to Creation, Jesus Christ brings to mankind Eternal Salvation.

THE CHURCH AND CRITICISM

The Church has the ability and is fully competent to adequately deal with the problem of modern criticism. The Church does not quite understand her power; she can fight a mighty battle if she wills to do it. The Church is a born fighter; she was conceived in conflict, and by conflict only can she triumph. The policy of silence and compromise that has too long prevailed is contrary to the genius of the Church, and because

of which divisions are appearing amongst us.
Next to peace, the Church should love nothing
better than conflict for God and His Truth. To
this we are called to-day, and we should ask, Have
we heard the call; have we enlisted; does the
world know where the Church stands? This is the
question that is pressing in from every quarter.
What are the churches going to do with the anti-
Christian movement in education in America?
Shall it be defeated? Shall we rise up into the
heights with God and believe Moses, Christ, and
Paul? These queries must be answered; they are
insistent; they will not be silenced; we cannot
dodge them; the struggle is truly on. What are
we going to do with the Bible; and what are we
going to do to destroy an apostate Christianity
and redeem our institutions for God?

THE GREATNESS OF THE PROBLEM

Separating Modernism from our institutions
and the churches is a task of the first magnitude,
because this false system is abetted and fortified
by the boast and power of material wealth. There
is a powerful financial concern that is laboring
to control the higher education of America. This
trust is devoting millions to the spread of Modernism in American education, in all those institutions where the false criticisms of the Bible are
rampant; and they are doing this with the knowledge and approval of many of the prominent laymen in the churches. These philanthropists are

members of the churches. Of course the churches
never thought it expedient to investigate the conduct of these men for supporting our educational
institutions. It probably never occurred to the
American people that to give millions to education
was an act that should call for church discipline.
It is rather a badge of honor, and of loyalty to the
highest and best. Should such an act be considered as worthy of investigation, the need of
money in the work of the local church, as in the
college, would prove the stronger appeal, and win
immunity for the benefactor of education. Moreover, many of the supporters of our institutions
are officers in local churches; thus their influence
there is two-fold—financial and official—and their
protection is doubly assured.

PERSONAL PRIDE AND FRIENDSHIP

There is also the element of personal friendship
to reckon with. It is hard to go back on a friend.
It is not to-day so much a question of loyalty
to the Bible; it is reduced to loyalty to a friend.
Jesus Christ is seldom taken into the consideration in this important matter. It is viewed as
something more important than even that—it is
loyalty to a rich man, or to some influential
friend! It is also, in many cases, friendship for
those in the pulpits who are advocates of the New
Theology. If the church happens to be fond of
their preacher, his winning personality, social
qualities, rhetoric, intellectual attainments then

all other considerations are discounted, for these are the things that count. It matters little whether the preacher is orthodox or heterodox, whether he accepts or rejects the Incarnation and Atonement of Christ for sin, whether he preaches or denies the Personal Coming of Christ, whether the Bible is to him inspired or not, these are matters of small concern, or at least not of the most important concern to many of the churches to-day. The great question is: Is the Pastor amiable, friendly, congenial with all, but especially with the "influential members?"

IGNORANCE TO DEAL WITH

There is also another and more serious element in our modern conflict over the Bible, and that is a lack of information on the part of the officials in the local churches. This is also true of the rank and file of the members. There is much lack of knowledge among the Church people generally as to the menace of the New Theology. And where ignorance is rife indifference is in the saddle. Many of the Christian people are so lacking in real knowledge of the Bible that they are incapable of knowing a New Theology sermon when they hear one. It is hoped that this volume will enlighten many, so that they will be able to detect even in the offing, the false in our literature, and in the teacher of Modernism.

DIFFICULTIES IN THE COLLEGE

What is true of the local churches is true also of the institutions of learning. Here personal friendships protect the teacher. The faculty is usually a close organization. As a member of a theological faculty recently said to the writer, "It is one thing to differ from another member of the faculty, but it is quite another matter to agitate his removal." It takes more strength of character to do that, more real "pep" than some of the teachers and Boards can muster. To the managing Boards of most of our institutions a teacher's loyalty to the Bible is not the most important matter. The teacher was engaged on his aptness to teach, his reputed scholarship, his degrees, and not on the basis of his knowledge of the Word of God and loyalty thereto. This is especially true of the university. In fact, the question as to whether the candidate is a person of piety is far from foremost in the minds of those whose work it is to engage instructors. At any rate, in most cases, his views as to Christian doctrines are not sought. If the candidate is passing decent, with a moral character, that is all the ethical and religious requirement. In some of our colleges are found noble exceptions to this rule. Nevertheless, it is not vital piety, but "modern scholarship" which means in most cases a college degree, and rejection of the Bible as the Word of God, that is the all important thing in many of our educational institutions.

Consequently, when some of our college and theological teachers slur and reject the supreme authority of the Bible, when they belittle the miraculous element, and refer to the parables of our Lord as "picturesque exaggerations," and His plain declarations about the lost as "cant," as do the advocates of Modernism, and claim that Jesus Christ himself was mistaken in certain matters, we can understand more clearly the seriousness of our problem. Furthermore, the student body, like those who make up the local churches, are, as a class, incapable of deciding for themselves whether the teacher is, in his instruction, true or false, right or wrong, Christian or anti-Christian. They are apt to gradually adopt his anti-Bible point of view.

Here then are a few of the obstacles that have to be encountered as earnest men and women contend for the Christian Faith in America. Personal friendships, indifference to Jesus Christ, rejection of the Bible as authority, the power of money, ignorance of the colossal evil of the anti-Bible teachings in many of our institutions of learning, and in many of the churches, and the lack of moral courage, on the part of many of the members of our churches, and among the boards and faculties, to deal adequately with infidelity in the guise of religion, or even to attempt to grapple with the biggest problem the Church has on her hands.

THE RISING STAR OF HOPE

But all these discouraging elements, these sad conditions that are obstacles to the progress of the Truth, can in time be overcome, and our churches and educational institutions be delivered from the blight of Modernism. We shall discuss the remedy later, but would here state that victory may be made complete. The reforms that a persistent religious education in pulpit, Sunday School, and elsewhere can bring to pass are beyond our power to fully comprehend. The weak and ignorant can be made wise and strong. The man of ill-gotten and unconsecrated wealth need not be the man of power. All teachers and preachers of Modernism can be disciplined, humbled, and silenced, and the educational institutions, and the local churches where it is taught, can be dealt with effectually. Churches that to-day are indifferent can be encouraged, enthused, enlightened, revived, and led forward in a heroic, spiritual, militant movement for God, His Kingdom and His Truth.

THE GREAT THINGS WE FORGET

It is clear to the most observant that America, with all her wealth and enlightenment, is in imminent danger of losing sight of her loftiest ideals. Money has taken the throne. We have been so busy gilding the framework that we have forgotten to look at the picture. This is a land of vast achievement. We have done grandly in the past; but we are in danger of losing our ethical ideals, our moral passion, and becoming a nation that has lost its vision, for money, and not God, is becoming more and more the touchstone of our thoughts and the lodestone of our ambitions.

GOD CAN SET US ASIDE

There is great danger that we shall forget God's plan. Possibly we forget how easily God can get along without us. Possibly we forget that Christianity was not born in Lombard Street or in Wall Street, but in a Manger, and that at the Advent of the Son of Mary, Heaven hung out a star in His honor and the angel choir sang a new song. Possibly we forget that it is Jesus Christ to-day and not the money centers that moves the world.

THE GREATEST POWER

When God wanted to introduce a new civilization He did not put His hand on a Rothschild, though He has some of His kings and queens among the rich, but on the slave-child Moses, earth's greatest law-giver, and the carpenter Jesus, earth's only Saviour, and the miner Luther, earth's greatest reformer. Possibly we forget that it is by the Cross of sacrificing love that the world will yet be saved, that millenniums after our present boasted civilization, with its pomp and glitter will have perished, the money barons,

who, to-day, are found among the enemies of the
Word of God, will have been forgotten like the
dust, while He who was once the Babe of the
Manger, the Carpenter of Nazareth, the despised
and Crucified on the accursed Tree, will be the
King of earth, and Monarch of all worlds; that
before Him every knee shall bow and every tongue
confess; that of him God's choirs will be singing:
"Unto Him that loved us and washed us from
our sins in His own blood, and hath made us kings
and priests unto God and His Father; to Him be
glory and dominion for ever and ever." (Rev.
1:5-6).

VICTORY IS COMING

The forces of righteousness must ultimately be
victorious in this conflict, for Jesus Christ never
lost a battle. God's eternal Truth must triumph!
For the Bible we have no fear; but we have a
great task, to awaken the churches to see the
danger of losing Christ. Many have fallen asleep
at the switch. The heroic spirit of the old pioneer
preacher whom President Jackson complimented
is needed to-day. The parson was booked to
preach where the great American was to stop over
night, and Andrew Jackson found himself in a
pew in the church. The deacons held a hurried
consultation, and calling the preacher from the
pulpit informed him of the presence of the President and requested him to be guarded in his
remarks.

Before beginning his message the preacher said: "I understand Andrew Jackson is with us and I have been requested to be guarded in my remarks. Andrew Jackson will go to Hell as quick as any other man if he does not repent."

At the close of the service the President stepped forward and said: "Sir, if I had a regiment of men like you I could whip the world." This is the courage needed.

Yes, victory is coming! Multitudes are awaking, and stirring times are ahead. These groups of praying saints all over this broad land are getting hold of the Power that moves the world. God is answering prayer. Fear and deep concern have taken hold of the managers of our institutions. Already, we can hear the sound of the footfalls of the coming victorious hosts. The rich man who recently pledged $100,000 to foreign missions but who withdrew the gift when he learned that the Board was going to send out young men fresh from a New York seminary, who denied the Virgin Birth, who advocated the "German Kultur" is typical of the growing spirit of a new and better day.

CHAPTER VI

WHAT IS MODERNISM?

MANY persons do not seem to know what the New Theology is. Of the two hundred and eleven college and university presidents from whom the writer received letters, discussing the modern religious problems, a number of these stated that they did not know what the New Theology is, while others said that there were numerous New Theologies, and that not any one of these was widely known and accepted. Not a few of these educators asked for information as to the New Theology.

In this chapter we shall label or fully describe this theology of Modernism in all its main outlines or features, presenting accurately its point of view, and fully explaining why this teaching is in conflict with the Word of God, in order that it may be known when heard or lectured about in schools and churches, or when seen in current literature. The New Theology has distinct features that are as marked in religion as is the Ethiopian racially.

We have already seen how this Theology got

136

here. Now we ask: How does it work, what does
it say and do, is it an improvement on the Old
Bible Theology, is it a blessing or a blight, shall
we retain it or reject it? This teaching is on our
hands, abroad in the land, prominent in our
education, demanding a hearing; what then shall
we do with it? The churches can no longer evade
this matter, but must face and answer this burning question.

BIBLE CLAIMS REJECTED

The first fact to be stated is, that the New
Theology is marked by its indifference to the
claims of the Bible. It denies any special inspiration for the Bible, in fact it denies inspiration as
to many of the books of the Bible. It never says
with the great prophets—"Thus saith the Lord,"
but it loves to affirm, "Thus says Emerson,
Spencer, Darwin, Rabbi Cohn, or the consensus
of scholarship, etc." It never predicates finality
to any statement simply because that statement
is found in the Bible. It does not hesitate to say
that the Apostles Peter and Paul may have been
mistaken. Some of these teachers affirm that the
Apostle Paul was the real founder of the Christianity of all the centuries up to about twenty-
five years ago, when the Christianity of Jesus was
discovered for the first time. They tell us that
"our task now is to get rid of the Apostle Paul,
with his doctrine of redemption by the death of
Christ and of justification by faith, for no truly

modern men believe these doctrines, and preach Jesus and His social Kingdom of human brother-hood.''

Here we find the New Theology dilemma. Most of these teachers claim that even Jesus Christ may have been mistaken, that he accepted at least the opinions current in His own day, especially those relating to the Old Testament and the man-ner of His Second Coming. This teaching would strip the Bible of its Supernatural authority and humanize, rationalize it, or make it appear to be a purely human product only, the result of a political and moral evolution, and not a book of joint authorship—God being the controlling fac-tor in its production. In brief, the New Theology treats the Bible largely as it treats any other highly ethical literature, picking and choosing certain parts as possibly inspired, independently of what the Bible writers claim for it, thus ex-alting man's reason as above God's Revelation.

It is clear, therefore, that the New Theology is at war against the Bible. It would view the Bible in the light of the twentieth century, and not the twentieth century in the light of the Bible. It would make the so-called principle of evolution the key to the interpretation of the Bible; while the Old Theology would make the Bible itself, plus the highest Christian experience, the key to its interpretation, believing with the old hymn writer that,

God is His own interpreter, and He will make it plain.

Advocates of the New Theology are experts at misrepresentating the grand old Book. One of their teachers recently ridiculed the idea of a serpent tempting our mother Eve, though the most ignorant Bible student could tell him that it was not a serpent but a beast of the field that tempted Eve, and that, as a result, God pronounced a judgment upon the beast and he became a serpent. (Gen. 3:1, 14, 15). ''Thou art cursed above all cattle and every beast of the field; and upon thy belly thou shalt go, etc.'' And the sight of a serpent ever suggests both God's hatred for man's sin and the enmity He put between this degraded beast, now a serpent, and the woman's seed.

IS THE BIBLE SELF-CONTRADICTORY?

Take another case. Modernists affirm that the Bible is self-contradictory, and refer to the various accounts of the inscription on the Cross, as recorded by all the evangelists, and yet differently by each; and also, as they affirm, the conflicting accounts of the resurrection of Jesus. ''How can such records be inspired?'' they ask. We shall submit the reply of Dr. James M. Gray as given in ''The Fundamentals,'' Vol. III.

It is to be remembered that the inscription was written in three languages calling for a different arrangement of the words in each case, and that one evangelist may have translated the Hebrew, another the Latin, while a third recorded the Greek! It is not said that any one gave the full inscription, nor can we affirm that there was any obligation upon them to do so. Moreover, no one contradicts any other, and no one says what is untrue. . . .   May not the Holy Spirit here have chosen to emphasize some one particular fact, or phase of a fact of the inscription for a specific and important end?   Examine the records to determine what this fact may have been.   Observe that whatever else is omitted, all the narratives record the momentous circumstance that the Saviour on the Cross was *The King of the Jews*.   Could there have been a cause for this? What was the charge preferred against Jesus by His accusers? Was He not rejected and crucified because He said He was the King of the Jews?   Was not this the central idea Pilate was providentially guided to express in the inscription?   And if so, was it not that to which the evangelists should bear witness?   And should not that witness have been borne in a way to dispel the thought of collusion in the premises?   And did not this involve a variety of narrative which should at the same time be in harmony with truth and fact?   And do we not have this very thing in the four gospels?

These accounts supplement but do not contradict each other. We place them before the eye in the order in which they are recorded.

THIS IS JESUS	THE KING OF THE JEWS
	THE KING OF THE JEWS
THIS IS	THE KING OF THE JEWS
JESUS OF NAZARETH	THE KING OF THE JEWS

The entire inscription evidently was, "This is Jesus of Nazareth, the King of the Jews," but we submit that the foregoing presents a reasonable argument for the differences in the records.

It is quite clear that Dr. Gray's argument is reasonable and unanswerable. Yet, as we have shown in Chapter III. Excerpts, etc., this position of Modernism as to the inscriptions on the Cross was taken by a New Theology student in his graduating thesis and was endorsed by the professor in Bible in that denominational college. It is amazing how ignorant some of these teachers are of the Bible.

REJECTION OF THE RESURRECTION

In referring to the fact of the resurrection of Christ at which some New Theology Modernists look askance, Dr. W. H. Griffith Thomas, of Wycliffe College, Toronto, Canada remarks:

It is well known that there are difficulties connected with the number and order of these appearances of Jesus, but they are probably due largely to the summary character of the story, and certainly are not sufficient to invalidate the uniform testimony to the two facts: (1) The empty grave, (2) the appearance of Jesus on the third day. These are the main facts of the combined witness.

The very difficulties which have been observed in the Gospels for nearly nineteen centuries are a testimony to a conviction of the truth of the narratives on the part of the whole Christian Church. The church has not been afraid to leave these records as they are, because of the facts that they embody and express. If there had been no difficulties, men might have said that everything had been artificially arranged, whereas the differences bear testimony to the reality of the event recorded. The fact that we possess these two sets of appearances—one in Jerusalem and one in Galilee—is really an argument in favor of their credibility; for if it had been recorded that Christ appeared in Galilee only, or Jerusalem only, it is not unlikely that the account might have been rejected for lack of support. It is well known that records of eye-witnesses often vary in details, while there is no question as to the events themselves. The various books recording the story of the

Indian mutiny, or the surrender of Napoleon III, at Sedan, are cases in point; and Sir William Ramsay has shown the entire compatibility of certainty as to the main fact with great uncertainty as to precise details. We believe, therefore, that a careful examination of the appearances will afford evidence of a chain of circumstances extending from the empty grave to the day of ascension. Thomas Arnold of Rugby said that "the resurrection was the best attested fact in history." . . . the Archbishop of Armagh stated that "the resurrection is the rock from which all the hammers of criticism have never chipped a single fragment." "There are five proofs of the resurrection: 1. The life of Jesus; 2. The Empty Grave; 3. The Transformation of the Disciples; 4. The Existence of the Primitive Church; 5. The Witness of St. Paul." (International Standard Bible Encyclopedia).

It seems, perhaps, unnecessary to discuss these historic and well-attested events, but it is only done to show what the New Theology is in its attitude toward the Bible, and how this school misrepresents the Book.

HOW MODERNISTS VIEW THE BIBLE

Modernists view the Bible very much as a kind of receptacle of documents, like the Patent Office, wherein is recorded the gradual evolution of man's inventions. Like the experts in the Courts they may give their opinions but it is the jury that must decide the case. When the experts disagree the jury takes the case out of their hands and decides it. It is well to remember that it is the average common-sense folk after all who must decide the character, merits and future of the Bible.

WAR ON THE MIRACULOUS ELEMENT.

The New Theology of Modernism belittles the miraculous element. To them miracles are not necessary to stamp the book as of God, in fact, to this school, miracles are rather an embarrassment. They affirm that if miracles occurred their purpose is restricted to the human ministry aspect only, and in no-wise serve as proof of the Divine authority of the Bible and the character of our Lord and His mission, though Jesus appealed to men to accept Him as the Son of God on the basis of His miraculous works. (John 5:36; 10:25; 14:11).

The miraculous element in both Old and New Testament most of the New Theology advocates deny; while the more bold amongst them openly repudiate miracles. The fact of a miracle presupposes a God working contrary to, or independently of evolution, or of any other supposed natural law; and to Modernists God does not thus work in any part of His universe, in contradistinction to the theory of evolution. They tell us that "modern scholarship" is agreed, that miracles must go, as if scholarship were ever agreed, or is capable of deciding the future of the Bible. As Dr. W. H. Griffith Thomas has well said:

Every fact must have an adequate cause, and the only proper explanation of Christianity to-day is the resurrection of Christ. The resurrection means the presence of miracle, and there is no evading the issue which confronts us, unless, therefore, we are prepared to accept the possibiltiy of the miraculous, all explanation of the New Testament and Christianity is a waste of time.

Dr. George P. Mains of The Methodist Book Concern has this to say in his defense of the radical criticism, in his book, "Christianity and the New Age:"

For the entire valuable process of emancipating the Bible from the fables of tradition, from unscientific dogma, from mystical and meaningless allegory . . . we are more indebted to the German than to any other single nation.

But these German scholars, however, made war on the miracles, the scholars whom Dr. Mains eulogizes in his book, as he says, scholars from, "Semler to Wellhausen." "These are the scholars who denied that Moses wrote the Pentateuch, and to whom, with all others of similar views, Dr. Green, late of Princeton University, in the opening words of the preface of, "The Unity of the Book of Genesis, says:"

All tradition, from whatever source it is derived, whether inspired or uninspired, unanimously affirms that the first five books of the Bible were written by one man and that man was Moses.   There is no counter-testimony in any quarter.

The New Theology of Modernism is at war to the hilt against the miraculous element in the Bible, or the Supernatural in the Christian Religion.

Canon Dyson Hague, M. A., of Wycliffe College, Toronto, in an article on the History of the Higher Criticism (by which

he means the destructive criticism) names a few of the most
conspicuous of the leaders of the movement as, Eichorn,
W. Vatke, George, Bleek, Ewald, Hupfeld, Graf, and Wellhausen.

They were rationalists whose views he gives
thus:

1. They denied miracles and the validity of any miraculous
narrative. Miracles were legendary and mythical.

2. They denied prophecy and the validity of any prophetical
statement. Prophecies were conjectures, coincidence, fiction,
or imposture.

3. They denied the reality of revelation. They were un-
believers of the supernatural. Their hypotheses were constructed on the assumption of the falsity of Scripture.

4. The Bible was a mere human product. It was a stage
in the literary evolution of a religious people. It was not
given by inspiration of God, and is not the Word of the living
God.—From the April number, *The Bible Champion*, N. Y.

As Dr. Mains is the Director General of Ministerial Education in the Methodist Episcopal
Church, it is evident that Methodism is getting,
to-day, through its younger ministers, a new and
serious inoculation of the deadly virus of the New
Theology of Modernism. This teaching will
change the spiritual character of this great denomination, if it has not already done so.

INTELLIGENT LAITY REPUDIATING THE NEW THEOLOGY

The New Theology has been having a rough
road to travel; they have been running up against
some disagreeable snags; they have been uncom-

fortably jolted; for science has been making a remarkable contribution on the side of the Bible. The spade has given eloquent testimony to the historicity of the Old Testament, especially to those parts which Modernists long ago repudiated, as stated clearly by Prof. George Frederick Wright, D.D., LL.D., of Oberlin, in "The Fundamentals," Vol. II.

In "The Identification of Belshazzar," the discovery of "the Moabite stone" (1868, see 2nd Kings, 3:4–27). "The expedition of Shishauk" (1st Kings, 14th Ch.) (which discovery corroborates the Old Testament) "The identification of Israel in Egypt of the city of Tähpan-hēs, (mentioned by Jeremiah) by the discoveries there in 1886 . . . known as the "Tel Defenueh" (Jer. 43:8) "The Store Cities of Python and Ramesis, discovered in 1883 confirmatory of the Book of Genesis" (Exo. 1:11 and Exo. 5) also the fact that the Pentateuch could only have been written in Moses' time." "The Tel El Amarna Tablets discovered in 1878 on the East bank of the Nile, containing numerous letters sent to the King of Egypt in 1300, showing that the four kings, mentioned in Genesis were real characters and not myths" (as modernists claim them to be) and numerous other historical facts prove beyond a doubt that the New Theology of Modernism has a very difficult road to travel, and serve to show why the most intelligent laymen and clergymen are repudiating it.

THE VIRGIN BIRTH AND CHRIST'S DEITY

The advocates of the New Theology say:

The two stories of the Virgin Birth entirely different from each other, and in hopeless conflict, are so preposterous that we cannot regard them as other than pure legend; and the stories of the resurrection are also legendary.

They do not point out their objections to the
Bible text and thus give reasons for such sweep-
ing statements. It is easy to make charges, but
furnishing proof is another matter. Prof. A. B.
Bruce, late of Glasgow University, said: "Rejection of the Virgin Birth seldom if ever goes by
itself. With it is apt to go denial of the virgin
life." In speaking of the difference in the two
narratives Dr. James Orr says:

Next to the Gospels they were not of late and non-apostolic
origin; but were written by *apostolic men,* and were from the
first accepted and circulated in the church as trustworthy
embodiments of sound apostolic teaching. Luke's Gospel was
from Luke's own pen—its genuineness has recently received a
powerful vindication from Prof. Harnack of Berlin—and
Matthew's Gospel . . . passed without challenge in the early
church as the genuine Gospel of the Apostle Matthew . . .
It is certain, that this Gospel in its Greek form always passed
as Matthew's . . . These narratives come to us, accordingly,
with high apostolic sanction.

In speaking of their sources Dr. Orr further
says:

Not a little can be gleaned from the study of their internal
character. Here two facts reveal themselves. The first is
that the narrative of Luke is based on some old, archaic, highly
original Aramic writing. Its Aramic character gleams through
its every page. In style, tone, conception, it is highly primitive—emanates apparently from that circle of devout people
in Jerusalem to whom its own pages introduce us (Luke 2:25,
36–38). It has therefore the highest claim to credit. The
second fact is even more important. A perusal of the narratives
shows clearly—what might have been expected—that the

information they convey was derived from no lower source
than Joseph and Mary themselves. This is a marked feature
of contrast in the narratives—that Matthew's narrative is all
told from Joseph's point of view, and Luke's is all told from
Mary's. The signs of this are unmistakable. Matthew tells
about Joseph's difficulties and action, and says little or nothing
about Mary's thoughts and feelings. Luke tells much about
Mary—even her inmost thoughts—but says next to nothing
directly about Joseph. The narratives, in short, are not
contradictory, but are independent and complementary. The
one supplements and completes the other. Both together are
needed to give the whole story They bear in themselves the
stamp of truth, honesty, and purity, and are worthy of all
acceptation, as they were held to be in the early church. The
genealogies present problems, but they do not touch the central
fact of the belief of Matthew and Luke in the birth of Jesus
from a virgin. . . . The silence of John and Mark as to the
Virgin Birth has its reasons. Mark begins with Christ's public
ministry, and John traces Christ's divine descent into Eternity
and says, "the Word became flesh," but he takes no time to
tell how this miracle was performed. He had the Gospels
of Matthew and Luke in his hands while he wrote, and he
takes the knowledge of their teaching for granted. To speak
of contradiction in a case like this is entirely out of the question.

Thus Dr. Orr has answered completely the
claims of Modernism that these narratives are
"hopelessly   contradictory . . . and   preposterous." Like the inscriptions on the Cross, and the
accounts of the various appearances of Jesus after
His resurrection, these narratives of the Virgin
Birth are not contradictory; they both tell the
truth, neither one denies what the other says.
Their apparent differences reveal their genuineness, that they were not a manufactured tale by

those who wanted to start a new religion. If it were the latter, or if they were legendary both accounts would agree in all matters of detail. They do agree perfectly in the great essential fact that Jesus was born of a virgin. As Dr. G. Campbell Morgan has well said:

The incarnation was necessary (1) to reveal the Father, (2) as a revelation of God to the Race, and (3) as a revelation to the individual. By it, as by the Cross, we see the working out into visibility of eternal things. The sorrow of God over man's sin and the joy of God over man's redemption are wrought out. God has now come very near to us in Christ. The meaning of the incarnation, as of the Cross, is that God suffers for his wayward children, that sin and suffering are co-existent as are joy and redemption.

We quote the following from "Consider Christ Jesus," by Rev. Daniel Hoffman Martin, of New York:

The Deity of Christ, like his resurrection, is one of the best attested facts in the life of Christ and in history. To do away with the Deity of Christ we would have to do away with the Bible portrait of Christ. The critics would try to cut out the supernatural features of the Bible. Is this conceit or ignorance? Are they of keener intellect than those who believe that portrait to be the handiwork of God? A child can cut out all the best pictures from the best books in the library and he need not be a very bright child either. Our fathers used their slippers on the advanced thinkers in their homes when they found us scissoring engravings from choice books. Our destructive critics, and would-be advanced thinkers, have not advanced one inch beyond the Jews of two thousand years ago who stoned the Apostles for proclaiming the Deity of Christ. Far from being somewhat new and modern and fresh and

up-to-date, the new Unitarianism is stale and moldy and moth-
eaten. It was repudiated in the Apostolic day, later in the
fourth century, and Americans are repudiating it to-day. The
impression which the life of Christ has made upon the world
can only be explained by the fact that He was more than man.

There is no soul-winning movements in the New
Theology of Unitarianism. There is not a New
Theology Unitarian rescue mission in the Universe. There is no great joyous Christian experience in this religion. Edward Everett Hale was
viewed as the patron saint of the New Theology
of Unitarianism in America. His son is reported
to have been converted to Christ in an orthodox
revival at Union College, and this is what he is
claimed to have said: ''I never knew that there
was such joy to be found in the belief that Jesus
is the Son of God and a personal Saviour.'' Young
Mr. Hale learned the secret of our Lord, of the
New life in Him, not from his father, but from
an orthodox evangelist. In speaking of his own
Deity our Lord said:

For the Father loveth the Son and showed Him all things
that Himself doeth: and He will show Him greater works than
these, that ye may marvel.

For as the Father raiseth up the dead and quickeneth them;
even so the Son quickeneth whom He will.

For the Father judgeth no man but hath committed all
judgment unto the Son.

That all men should honor the Son even as they honor the
Father.

He that honoreth not the Son honoreth not the Father which
hath sent him. (John 5:20–23.)

Dr. Martin says further:

Nearly a century ago Channing launched his New Theology movement in Boston. Harvard and its Professors went over, as did the aristocracy of Beacon Street. Philosophers, poets, and people of wealth became Modernists in many parts of New England. But what do the nearly 100 years show us? The few Congregational churches in New England that remained true to the Deity of Jesus to-day have a membership of 700,000 while the Unitarians claim 70,000.

At the time of Channing, the Baptists and Methodists had only a few hundred thousand members each, while to-day these Churches have each about 7,150,000, according to the latest census printed by an officer of the Southern Baptist Convention. About thirty years ago one of the best known Unitarian New Theology Ministers in New York said to a Baptist clergyman there, "Within a generation we shall capture New York." But what has happened? New York City has grown to 6,000,000 and now it has fewer Unitarian churches, only four in all.

We quote again from Dr. Martin:

Multiply what the evangelical churches have done and you have a girdle of light encircling the globe. How many missionaries have the Unitarian New Theology of Channing sent out to the dark places of the earth? Five hundred? Guess again. Four hundred? Try again. Three hundred? Two hundred? One hundred? Ten? Five? One? No, not a single missionary in pagan lands representing this Unitarian New Theology. I am not throwing stones. I recognize worth wherever I find it. I am stating facts. The doctrine of a human

Christ produces a visionless religion. The test of a religious teaching is its producing energy. Even Dr. Channing in his old age said: "I would that I could look to Unitarianism with more hope," and Edward Everett Hale in his old age said: "I cannot see why so simple and democratic a religion as Unitarianism has not swept the country long ago." Rev. Dr. Jefferson of New York says that the question was answered by Gamaliel who told the Sanhedrin when the Apostles were arrested for preaching the Deity of Christ. "If this work be of man it will come to naught, but if it be of God you cannot overthrow it lest you be found fighting against God." This is simply the scientific law of the survival of the fittest.

How often have I seen in my lifetime ethical temples dedicated to religion with Christ as God left out. They have flourished for a little while and then their doors are closed forever. Their laws for good order and right living have never taken hold of men. I have known able men who, espousing the cause of Unitarian New Theology gathered large congregations. Where are those churches now? Dissolved into powder and blown away. Beecher preaching the Deity of Christ, built up a great church, and it is as great to-day. Joseph Parker, as brilliant, built up a great church, but its congregation disappeared at his death.

Our young people and other good-meaning souls wonder what is the difference between Unitarianism, New Theology, and Orthodox Christianity, for they seem to see good people in both. The vital difference between the two is, one is a pool, the other is a spring. A pool is fed from without while a spring is fed from within. A Unitarian or New Theology church can never exist by itself in any community. Their ministry is to members of other churches. Wherever it does exist you will find that its life is fed by the other churches around it.

Let us not be fooled by such catch phrases as "salvation by character." Salvation into character by the power of the living Christ is the only Gospel.

Only those who do not know their Bible and

Jesus Christ as a personal Saviour are accepting the results of the radical criticism and the New Theology. The most thoughtful, the real Bible students are asking questions, studying their Bibles, examining the teachings of Modernism with the wise and inevitable result that the ablest Bible students everywhere are declaring that the New Theology is a false, worthless, deceptive thing, that its speculations, hypotheses, denials of the Word of God, and doubt engendering propaganda must be repudiated, as it has been exposed and defeated all along the line.

DEIFICATION OF MAN

Another mark of the New Theology. It would deify human nature and affirm that man by nature is a true, pure child of God, needing only a proper education to fully develop his character and make him fit for earth and Heaven, consequently, the fact and need of regeneration by the Holy Spirit of God are winked at. A message is seldom if ever heard from this school on this important requirement of God's Word, or if heard is of such a character that it contains no positive affirmation as to the necessity of this fundamental change or experience in man's life.

To the New Theology salvation is by education and not by moral regeneration. This accounts for the fact that advocates of Modernism give their support not so much to missions and worldwide evangelization, to the Christianization of the world, and the enthronement of Jesus Christ in the hearts of men, as to the colleges where reason is enthroned and Jesus Christ is often dethroned, and to those social institutions of a semi-religious character that have not in them a distinct Gospel message.   Churches that are controlled by this school eschew the warm-hearted Gospel evangelistic preacher, for such a messenger would be too positive, constructive, aggressive, and hence a constant irritant on the sensibilities of the advocates of the New Theology.   Man, to them, is a little god, and can be educated and evolved into the ideal, aside from the help of the distinctive teachings of the Christian religion, and the vitalizing saving life of Jesus Christ.

ANTIPATHY TO EVANGELISM

The antipathy of Modernism to evangelism should be specially noted.   Slurs at consecrated evangelists are some of their most common stock in trade, notwithstanding the fact that the Christian Church was established in a revival of religion by the world's greatest evangelistic preacher, Jesus the Christ.   Not being able to bring about revivals of religion, the adherents of Modernism would conceal their impotence in this regard by slurring or belittling the work of the God-appointed men who are used of the Holy Spirit to bring about revivals of religion.   The

WHAT IS MODERNISM? 155

fact that this type of preacher and teacher cannot bring to pass revivals of religion in the churches and in the colleges is one of the strongest indictments against the New Theology.

When the critics can produce revivals of true religion the author will apologize to them and withdraw this message from circulation. And this is not, as Mark Twain would say, "writ sarcastic," but stated as an earnest protest against this abomination in our education and churches. How can this thing win a sinner from the error of his ways? What is there in it to win? Can its criticisms, negations, ethical principles, lack of humility, rejection of the inspiration of the Bible, of the atonement and deity of Christ, air of assumed intellectual superiority, denial of man's lost and hopeless state in sin, produce conversions in the churches and educational institutions, or revivals of true religion? The result of the teaching of a lofty idealism, and not a Divine Dynamic, or the Christ, is the very antithesis, both in its content and results, of holy revivals of true religion. The antipathy of Modernism to evangelism would negative any effort in which they might engage to win men to Jesus Christ.

THE PRAYER-MEETING

If we examine the church-prayer service where this compromise is taught what do we discover? Not the converts of the New Theology engaged in testimony and prayer, for these men have no spiritual converts. Those who keep alive the prayer-meeting, as all other spiritual service, are the converts of the Old Theology of Calvary. If we go to the rescue missions here also the same facts are in evidence. Who are the men who are laboring there? Why do the redeemed from the lowest depths of degradation always attribute their salvation to the power of the Saviour's blood? Tell one of these that he may be saved by the development of his character, and he is not too benighted to see through this colossal falsehood. As well might an army endeavor to conquer America with soft mud for shells as Modernists attempt to win men to Christ by denying salvation through the atoning blood. Men intuitively know that they cannot save themselves, that by nature their tendencies are toward evil more than toward God, and that what they need is a spiritual power to reach them and redeem them from sin—they need a Saviour, Teacher, Helper, Comforter, an ever-present Friend.

SALVATION BY CHARACTER

Closely akin to the above is another mark of Modernism, to wit: that man is saved by the inherent goodness of his own character, as expressed in conduct or social service. In this the work of the Holy Spirit of God is denied, and Jesus is superfluous. This school does not believe that "salvation is of the Lord," but by doing good deeds; Jonah, however, believed it, for when he found himself at the "bottom of the mountains and the earth with her bars about him" (Jonah 2:6) he cried and said: "Salvation is of the Lord." And let our dealer in social platitudes get into a tight place, like Jonah, where human help is unavailing, and he also will cry, "Salvation is of the Lord." As Spurgeon said: "The one who believes in salvation by character, by good works, is a Calvinist when he prays." David had the vision of Jesus, when he said that "a fire was kindled against Jacob . . . because they believed not in God, and trusted not in his salvation," (Ps. 78:21-22). The Apostle Paul referred to those who teach salvation by man's natural character when he. wrote, "For they being ignorant of God's righteousness, and going about to establish their own righteousness, have not submitted themselves unto the righteousness of God." (Rom. 10:2). The Christian will be rewarded for his good works (Luke 8:35) but he is delivered from his sins by the sovereign grace of God through Christ (Rom. 4:45) (Eph. 1:7; 2:5). If those who trust in their righteousness could but get a glimpse of their own hearts, of the character of their thoughts, and of the holiness of God, doubtless they would quickly change their emphasis from character to grace, and say in real sincerity, with Isaiah: "But we are all as an unclean thing and all our righteousness is as filthy rags," (Isa. 64:6) or with the Apostle Paul,

"There is none righteous, no not one," (Rom. 3:10). The teaching that denies to the great God the work of saving men and making them righteous is a sad deception, but this is what the New Theology is doing; its salvation is a poor prop, a human effort, a mere "aspiration toward the ideal," with no Power to keep the soul from lapsing into its own helplessness and guilt and death.

NO REMEDY FOR SIN

Again, Modernism talks fluently about sin, denounces sin in the church, in society, in the nation, calls upon literature and experience to back up its indictment of sin, and yet at the moment, when it has shown the problem of evil, its hands fall limp, its lips are dumb, it closes the discussion without one true and effective word as to the remedy. The teacher of the New Theology can make a diagnosis, and, in part, tell what the trouble is with this world; and he assumes that he has a cure; but when he ought to apply the remedy he finds he has none. O yes, he does counsel men to wash up, to clean their tenements, to pay their debts—splendid advice, for honesty and sanitation are good things. It is well to keep wholesome, to "help the under dog," to wash the poor neighbor's baby, to think and act socially, but all these things may not be a part of salvation at all; they ought to be a part of the result of salvation. No, this is not the remedy for sin and its guilt. Our social good deeds cannot wash this foul thing away, for when we have done our best, our sins, our guilt will still cry out in the quiet hours and disturb our sleep. No remedy, no remedy, for sin!

THE AWFUL TRADEGY

Here is the awful tragedy of it! Think of it, a preacher of Christianity with no remedy for sin! True, these Modernists speak to men the great Master's loving words, "Come unto me . . . and I will give thee rest" (Matt. 11:28). But how shall they come to this Great Friend? What is the way by which they may come to Him? Silence! What must the sinning ones do and believe in order to come to Jesus Christ? Profound silence! How do men know that their sins are forgiven? A silence like unto death!

"But," some one may say: "Do they not tell about the power of the blood?" Tut, tut, my friend, where have you been living during the last twenty years? Surely not in America, or you must have been religiously asleep. Do you not know that these New Theology advocates shudder at the thought of the blood of Jesus as having made an atonement for sin and guilt? If they could only see it and feel the love-power there is in it! If they could only say deep down from the bottom of their hearts, "The blood of Jesus Christ, God's Son, cleanseth us from all sin," (I John 1:7) "And . . . He is the propitiation '(atonement) for our sins . . . and for those of the whole world.'' (I John 2:12) or, ''Who Himself bare our sins in his own body on the tree,'' (I Pet. 2:24-25), or some other sweet word of the Gospel, as ''God so loved the world that he gave his only begotten Son, that whosoever believeth on him should not perish but have everlasting life'' (John 3:6), then we should drop our pen and rejoice with great joy!

THE CROSS NOT SUPREME

But alas such is not the case. The Cross is not in the thinking of these men. At this Supreme Place in history they part company with the redeeming Christ. Such words as redemption, atonement, legal, sin-bearer, substitution, propitiation, which reveal the fathomless love of God for men, they have tried to rule out of our religious vocabulary. These words presuppose a Fall and a deep need, but how could there be a Fall in the scheme of evolution? Though the law of sacrifice is written all over the face of nature—one planet gives itself for another planet —though the sun is slowly burning himself out and some day he will be a corpse nailed to a cross, though the principle of our Lord's death is illustrated on battlefields, in the family, society, the nation, the world, though the mother gives herself for her child, the lover for the object of his affections, the patriot for his country, and men everywhere die that others may not die, and

suffer that others may not suffer, yet it matters
not to the teachers of Modernism. Is it not amazing how these men recoil from the great love
which reveals to us the heart of God? "Do not
tell us," they say, "of the blood of Christ; tell
us of the example of Christ." But the blood is
still there! "Tell us of the influence of Christ."
But the blood is still there! "Tell us of the
humanity of Christ." But the blood is still there!
We cannot get away from it! We must give up
Jesus Christ and throw the Bible to the winds,
if we reject the precious blood of the Cross!

HOW LOVE IS SHOWN

We cannot tell of God's love apart from Jesus'
blood. Shall we dare talk about it and shut our
eyes to what that love came into our world to do?
Here is the scriptural way of making known the
love of God. "I live by the faith of the Son of
God who loved me and gave himself for me."
(Gal 2:20). "I do not frustrate the grace of
God. For if righteousness come by the law then
Christ died in vain." (2:21). In other words,
if we reject the fact of our Lord's death for the
world's sin we are rejecting the love of God. As
the beloved Apostle John, who knew much about
the tender heart of Jesus, said: "In this is manifested the love of God toward us, because that
God sent his only begotten Son into the world
that we might live through Him. Herein is love"
—and I imagine I hear John's voice swell in a

holy rising inflexion, and see his eyes glow with a great emotion, as he says it—"Herein is love, not that we loved God, but that He loved us and sent His Son to be the propitiation (atonement) for our sins" (I John 4:9, 10).   The world's richest treasures come as result of sacrifice.   We boast of the Constitution, but it was the price of blood, heart blood, red blood that we paid for it.

IS THE ATONEMENT A FAILURE?

Modernism says: "The atonement has been worked to death."   But it is not worked at all, rather it is ridiculed or forgotten.   Here is the calamity of modern Christianity: God cannot use the preachers' message for there is no Cross in it.   Let the atonement be worked, or better, let it be tenderly and lovingly presented and our slumbering churches will be revived, our educational institutions will enjoy the gentle dews of heaven, and Protestantism will stop confessing failure on any field.   Work the death of the Christ and we shall witness the triumphs of the true Church, for men will then see their sins in the light of both God's wrath and His Love, and will fall at Jesus' feet, and crown Him Lord of all.

FATHERHOOD AND BROTHERHOOD

Another mark of the New Theology is found in its teaching regarding the Fatherhood of God and brotherhood of man, teaching a Fatherhood and brotherhood where the Scriptures reveal there is neither. Doubtless, the Fatherhood of God is taught in the Bible, but it is always confined to those who are in harmony with the Father, in fellowship with Him, who have cut loose from sin, and is never based on the fact that God has a claim upon all men as their Creator. If the latter is the rightful basis for the Fatherhood of God then Satan could also claim sonship. Creation is not the ground for this great doctrine; rather it is found in both God's holiness and in a certain type of spirit in man. The relationship cannot be claimed without the moral affinity, or better, the moral union of both parties. But in order to enter into this relationship there must first be a change on man's part. He must get a vision. The New Testament abounds in proof of this. "No man can say that Jesus is the Lord but by the Holy Ghost," is one way of expressing this fact; and "Except a man be born from above he cannot see the Kingdom of God" is another way of stating it. "For as many as are led by the Spirit of God they are the sons of God," makes clear that the fact of sonship is conditioned upon a holy life. For further references see II Cor. 6:16-18, John 8:38-42, Mark 3:35, John 1:12-13, Col. 1:13.

NO SALVATION IN NATURAL BROTHERHOOD

The natural brotherhood of man is good so far as it goes, but it has in it elements of evil and cannot solve the social and spiritual problems of our race.   In Matthew 15:19 our Lord makes clear the spirit of the natural man: "For out of the heart proceed evil thoughts, murders, adulteries, fornications, thefts, false witnesses, blasphemies."   Every man has in him the elements by nature which, if developed, would make him a murderer.   These Modernists who talk about the divinity of human nature, man a son of God by natural birth, etc., lock their doors at night, believe in safety vaults, and laws to curb and punish, and know that man outside the constraining and controlling love of God, and the restraint of human laws, is not to be trusted.   Let them be as reasonable and wise in matters of religion, and emphasize the new spiritual brotherhood in Christ as the hope of the world, for only in Christ are men true brothers, as only in Christ is God our Father.

This, however, in no-wise involves a denial of the fact that man in his personality was originally made in the image of God.   The presence of sin has effected a separation, and loss of moral likeness to God; consequently, instead of love, selfishness has become the dominating power in man's natural life.

THE CHARACTER OF GOD'S FAMILY

There is also involved in the New Testament teaching of the Fatherhood of God and the brotherhood of men in Christ, the honor, rights

and dignity of the heavenly family. I want no
one to tell me that John Smith is my brother,
for I know who are my brothers, as I also know
who is my father. To say that Smith is my
brother would be an incrimination of the character of my father. And as human families have
their lines of demarkation, and clearly defined
laws and characteristics, so likewise has the great
redeemed family of God. There is here the
logical, and may we say, the natural exclusiveness
of the new moral type of man in Christ, of that
which the Apostle Paul calls the "new creation;"
—"If any man be in Christ he is a new creation,"
a distinct new type in which he finds himself a
real brother to every member of the mystical
Body of Christ, be he black, white, or yellow.
They are all one. They are brothers in Christ and
can address God, as, "Our Father." They have
all been baptized by the Holy Spirit into one
Body, and hence, are now fully entitled to the
privileges and honors of the new brotherhood of
the Kingdom of God. No proper interpretation
of the parable of the prodigal son and the disciples' prayer will deny these facts. The latter
was intended for disciples, obedient children only,
while the former illustrates how a wayward son
may be restored, one who was already a son, and
the superabundance of the forgiving love of God.
A world baptized in human blood does not present
the true brotherhood, that God's Son came to
create, but rather the type of brotherhood He

came to destroy, and in its place to build up the new brotherhood of man—the Kingdom of God. Let social reformers, statesmen, writers, yes, and let preachers also put the emphasis here, and rally sinning, selfish, unbrotherly men to Jesus Christ. This is the shortest and only route to social, as it is to individual happiness and peace.

A FATAL DEPARTURE

Of the departure of the New Theology at this point from the true Gospel, men should everywhere be informed. We should not have dwelt at such length on this matter were it not of great importance to correct thinking and teaching. But the Modernist, being an evolutionist, has no place in his philosophy of man and human development for "a new creation" in Christ. With him it is first the germ, then the organism, then the lower form of physical life, then the animal, and finally the human-animal, possessing some moral qualities which call for cultivation or education, or improvement. This is, to him, the best we have, man's only hope of salvation. He has lost sight of the new born man, under the influences of Christ, and of the New Testament revelation of the same. He wipes out all distinctions between men of a moral and spiritual character. To him there should be no line of separation between the Church and other folks, for he sees no great regeneration, no moral change. There is only an age-long struggle and growth. But in this message we are chiefly concerned with the authority of Scripture and the facts of human experience. We have no desire to take from men any splendor of natural qualities, but rather to place the emphasis where God has placed it, on the fact and glory of the "new creation," the new brotherhood in Christ. "For whosoever shall do the will of God, the same is my brother, and my sister, and mother." (John 3:35).

THE KINGDOM OF GOD

Still another mark of the New Theology is its denial of the coming in governmental and visible form of the Kingdom of God upon earth, contending as they do, that God's Kingdom is ever a mystical unseen reality, and that this term, the Kingdom of God, always means character, and nothing more than the building up among men of the Christian type of manhood in the world. They affirm that the only significance of this term, the coming of the Kingdom, is the gradual increase in the number of Christ's disciples, and that the Kingdom will be here universally when every member of the human race will have been converted to Christ.

IMPOSSIBLE INTERPRETATION OF THE KINGDOM

But the New Testament is silent as to this interpretation of the coming of the Kingdom of God. Surely if this is what is meant, it will take a long long time for the Kingdom to become a universal reality, as there are millions more births of non-Christians yearly, in the world, than there are additions to the number of the disciples of Christ. After nearly 2000 years of Gospel work among non-Christians there still remains four-fifths of the human family unconverted. It is plain from these facts that the Kingdom of God will never become universal if the above is the way it is to be brought in. It is high time that Christians were apprised of this fallacious teaching of Modernism, as to the coming of the Kingdom of God, and taught the real facts as they are revealed in the Scriptures.

THE CHURCH AND KINGDOM

We are now in the Church age, when the great program is not to bring in the Kingdom, in the sense in which this term is usually meant, but to preach the Gospel to all peoples everywhere, to call out a people for His Name, to cooperate with the Holy Spirit in building up the Body of Christ, by preaching and witnessing for Him. God has nowhere promised that the whole world would be converted to Christ, but he directs that all men be given an opportunity to be saved. Indeed our Lord foresaw clearly that many would refuse salvation, and even that in the latter period of this Church age there would be a time of great falling away from the Christian faith (Luke 18:8). In Matt. 13:24-30, 36-40, it is made clear that the tares and wheat are to grow together until the time of harvest, or the end of the age. In other words many will remain unsaved to the end when they will be separated. "Lord wilt thou at this time restore the Kingdom to Israel?" (Acts 1:6) said the anxious disciples to Jesus, just before His ascension into glory. And He replied: "It is not for you to know the times or the seasons which the Father hath put in his own power," indicating plainly that there would be introduced a Divine Theocracy, a heavenly Kingdom on earth at some future time, nevertheless, their great work, after His departure, was not to bring in that Kingdom, but to evangelize the nations. Thus Jesus added: "But ye shall receive power, after the Holy Ghost is come upon you, and ye shall be witnesses unto me . . . unto the uttermost part of the earth." (Verse 8.)

THE KINGDOM AND HUMAN BODIES

Probably no words as to the character of the Kingdom of God could be plainer than the Apostle's declaration in I Cor. 15:50, "Now this I say brethren that flesh and blood cannot inherit the Kingdom of God," as much as to say, the possession of the Kingdom of God includes the new resurrection body, the body of immortality. But Modernists deny this resurrection body, hence they must teach, in order to be true to their evolutionary hypothesis, the presence of the Kingdom of God in the world to-day, that it is now inherited by flesh and blood or human bodies. The character of the Kingdom body was given in type on the Mount of Transfiguration when Jesus was transfigured before Peter, James and John. It is a body of beauty, of power and glory—an immortal or deathless body.

AN IMPORTANT DISCRIMINATION

"But what," we may inquire, "do all these passages signify which refer to the Kingdom of God?" Upon a close examination of these it will be found that there is what may be called, a two-fold manifestation of the Kingdom. First, there is the manifestation, in a measure to-day, in this Church age, of the Spirit of the Kingdom. Every true child of God possesses this Spirit, this Holy Christian Spirit, the Spirit who creates faith and hope and love, and "joy and peace in the Holy Ghost"—the Kingdom spirit in man.

This Holy Spirit gives us the foretaste or earnest of the great and glorious manifestation of the Kingdom, which will occur at the Coming of Our Lord Jesus Christ. The Spirit of God is ever the Spirit of the Kingdom of God in every age and world. So we can truly say, the Kingdom of God, in this sense, is within us, is possessing us, that is, we have its Spirit. But it should not be forgotten that it is also this same Spirit which makes us "heirs of the Kingdom" and gives us the earnest of our inheritance. The Apostle James refers to this heirship when he said by way of encouragement to those saints who were poor in this world's goods: "Hath not God chosen the poor of this world rich in faith and heirs of the Kingdom which he hath promised to them that love him," (James 2:5) the Kingdom that had not then been manifest on this earth.

It is for this great Kingdom the Holy Spirit is now preparing the Bride of Christ. We have the Kingdom Spirit now, and it is in this sense only that we can say, we are in the Kingdom. We are heirs of it, as it shall be manifested at our Lord's return. Then the Kingdom, for the first time, will have been seen in its true glory and in its governmental form upon this planet. The glorious King himself shall be here and reign in person. We should have this in mind when we pray, "Thy Kingdom come," as well as the immediate regeneration by the Spirit of the sons and daughters of men. The coming Kingdom of Glory, with the triumphant King, is the needed vision for the Church to-day. (See II Tim. 4:1; Luke 22:29-30; Luke 23:42; John 18:36).

THE SECOND COMING OF CHRIST

The last mark of Modernism we would mention only, is its antagonism to the doctrine of our Lord's return. At this great truth these friends almost rave like mad-men. They have exhausted our language in search of words with which to express their antipathy to this glorious revelation

in God's holy Word. They say that "this doctrine is cataclysmic, destructive, sensational; that
it is built on apocalyptic language; that all who
believe it are cranks, with a mental twist, not
wholly reliable and level-headed persons," etc.,
etc. They look with pity, bordering on contempt,
upon those who teach it, and those who support it.
No space will be given here to a treatment of
this marvelous revelation. We shall reserve this
discussion for the chapter on The Second Coming of Christ, as given in, *The Modern Conflict
Over the Bible.*

CHAPTER VII

THE REMEDY—EDUCATION AND REFORMATION

IT is generally believed that Germany's downfall is the result of her departure from the Evangelical Faith. Her criticism of the Bible and atheistic philosophies have done their work. This we believe is now demonstrated before the whole world; and it requires no argument to sustain this fact.

It is also known that these same powerful influences in education are entrenched in our American institutions of learning, that our system of education is shot through with anti-Christian propaganda, that the unproved theory of evolution is the guiding principle in almost every study in our schools. This also needs no elaboration, no prolonged argument, for it is known by all well-informed persons.

The writer recently gave an address before the students and faculty of one of our theological seminaries, where he had an occasion to hear a teacher (who by the way was the President of the University) conduct his class in "The Elements of Psychology." The text-book used was nothing more or less than an elaboration of the theory of evolution as the author tried to apply it to the development and laws of mind. And the teacher spun out his wise nonsense to the students, as if he were revealing one of the most important facts in human life. But this is true of almost every teacher in philosophy and science in most of our universities to-day, so completely have these institutions gone over to Modernism, or as a recent writer calls it—"paganism." The Standard Dictionary defines paganism as idolatry. It means any system of belief that is opposed to Christianity, that is, to salvation by the merits and work of Christ. Paganism, therefore, means salvation by man's efforts and good works. What we want to do is to assure those who have not as yet learned this fact, in order that they may know what is their responsibility in cooperating with others, in helping to strike the blow that shall set our institutions free.

REMEDY IN EDUCATION

We shall ask, What is the remedy? We shall now take up one of the most momentous questions in our world to-day, namely: How shall America rid herself of the New Theology and its causes, of the philosophies and criticism of the Bible that brought about the downfall of Germany, and thus conserve and perpetuate Christianity in this country and the whole world. "As goes America so goes the world."

AMERICAN INFLUENCE

In a large and important sense America will soon become the center of the world—financially, politically, commercially, if it is not all that already. It is more important to make and keep America Christian, especially in our centers of education, than it is, for example, to conduct even our great foreign missionary enterprises, for if the fountain head is poisoned, all our missionary and civilizing work must suffer collapse. If the foundation is decaying the building will crumple. Indeed, this is what we are already witnessing on some of our foreign mission fields as result of the influences at work in our institutions at home.

NEW THEOLOGY ON MISSION FIELDS

The testimony of one of the oldest and best known among the missionaries of the China Inland Mission is worthy of notice. He said: "I visited a city in China where I heard one of the recent missionaries from the United States, a graduate of a New York Seminary, address a crowd in the market square. I was struck by the interest the natives were showing in what the missionary was saying. 'We are all alike. All men are religious. And there is truth in all religions. The great thing in all our religions is ethics. Be good, do good, that is all there is to it.' And the Chinese were nodding their heads on every side and smiling their hearty approval of the Christian missionary, who came over to tell them about ethics. They were heard to say: 'Just like us. Just like us.'" They treated the message as a joke. The joke was that any one should come so far to tell them what they themselves probably knew more fully than the speaker.

This cartoon is used by courtesy of the Christian Workers' Magazine, Chicago, Ill.

Keep him from the mission fields.

This is the type of messenger that not a few of our seminaries are creating to go to preach to the heathen. Jesus Christ is not absolutely essential. There is no Cross, no new birth, no real salvation in it.

SHOULD FIND A SOLUTION.

What is the remedy? This is the question that calls for an answer. It is no exaggeration to say that the future security of all our social, financial, educational, and religious structure will be largely determined by the way America answers this question. Do we want America to continue to be a Christian nation in the truest, the highest sense, or shall we permit this great country to become pagan? Do we want a prolonged peace, or shall we witness horror upon horror, paroxysms of bewilderment and despair, anarchy and social revolution? We are not putting these alternatives too strongly. Shall we cherish that which poisoned the educational and religious life of Germany, and that resulted in the collapse of that mighty nation, or shall we reject this menace to our social and religious well-being? If our answer is the latter, then it will devolve upon us to begin at once a work of reformation.

We must wake up America to see the peril that confronts us.

We must organize and mobilize the Evangelical Forces in order to destroy the anti-Christian influences in our educational and religious life.

In order to purify the institutions where Modernism is taught we must discipline and reform these institutions.

The management of the local churches must be taken in hand by men and women of proper

Bible education, of iron will, of loyalty to the Truth, and the pulpits must be protected from the New Theology.

These essential things may be classified as Education, Reformation, Organization.

EDUCATION AND AGITATION

This is the seed germ of all healthy reform. Agitation was the secret of the destruction of slavery, and will surely result in the defeat of the liquor traffic. Wise folks shake their heads and say: "Impossible, impossible," but the liquor traffic, like slavery, will be abolished.

The agitator is usually the crank, the man with the unchristian temper, the unbalanced enthusiast, as his enemies say; but he is the hero of the next generation. He is the seer, the prophet, the man of vision, of wide reaching and far seeing out upon the eternal. Listen thoughtfully to the agitator, whose soul is on fire in a great cause, for he is our greatest benefactor. He is worthy of a monument to mark the spot where his dust sleeps.

A GENERAL COOPERATION

Let every one who sees the need and hears the call, agitate against the New Theology in his own circle, his own home, his church, his place of work, whether he be a preacher, teacher, doctor, lawyer, or in professional work of any kind, or in the most humble toil. Let each one feel that he is called of God to help inaugurate a new day of spiritual freedom, a great national awakening against the false philosophies, the radical criticisms of the Bible, the pagan religious teachings as taught in the schools and in many of the pulpits of America, and thus lead the people into the possession of a warm, glowing, positive faith.

EDUCATE BY LITERATURE

Let this education he conducted wisely, tactfully, but fearlessly. Let each one who has the vision of the new imperative task be fortified with the best literature available on this momentous question, and distribute it continuously and generously. The new paganism is trying to enslave America with their false philosophies and science, by a wide circulation of their literature in our Sunday School publications, our magazines and newspapers. Let us be more wise and flood America with the best literature against the apostasy.

ONLY TWO ROADS

It must be made clear that there are only two roads for a nation to travel, and that we are now at the parting of the ways, in fact that many have gone beyond the parting.

One of these ways means love for God and service for men, a continuous improvement, an advance in all that is truest, noblest, best. It means that the present is secure and the horizon of our future golden with hope. It means a continuous revival of true religion, a moral regeneration that results in a richer, stronger fellowship and brotherhood, social and spiritual betterment, an advance in true education, true science and art, an improvement in the status and conditions of labor in every sphere, and a more equal distribution of wealth. It means national and individual happiness and peace—that shall crown and glorify us as a nation. This is what we must impress upon men as we educate, agitate, and push our holy propaganda for God.

But this is not true of the other road. Germany, and other nations also, furnish us with a partial illustration of the results of the rejection of the Bible as the Word of God. It means social unrest, rejection of the authority of Jesus Christ, war, revolution, the revival of autocracy and anarchy, the reign of lawlessness and brute force, the thwarting of vision, the annihilation of hope and love. Which way shall we travel? Momentous issues hinge on our decision. All this we should make plain in our agitation and education.

As a nation we feel smug and secure in our geographical isolation from the rest of the world, but we forget that we cannot get away from the impartial and unceasing operation of moral laws. Our future is not assured. We have heard the boast: "No nation would dare attack America." But our danger is not from without, but from within. A nation's greatest enemies may be of her own household. Our growing peril is not "the yellow peril," it lurks at our firesides, it centers in our universities, it is an apostate movement in the realm of education and religion.

IS REVOLUTION OUR LOT?

Some of the most far-seeing students of our times, both in the world of organized labor and finance, tell us that our political sky is not free from portents of a coming storm. Already many affirm that they can hear the whispers and see the signs of an approaching social revolution, that labor will rise against capital, and that blood will flow in these streets of ours, and the hearts of millions will be wrung with grief.

The public suspicions that existed in Europe for decades, as to the present war, at last proved to be prophetic. The deluge broke, and the Prussian apostasy in religion baptized our world in blood. And these symptoms of social unrest here are prophetic. They warn us to put our house in order. They cry aloud to the people of this nation to study the causes of our threatened destruction and remove them. Here then is cause for a nation-wide agitation, to purify our institutions of those anti-Christian influences that may later add fuel to the fire. We must purify the springs of national life, our education, and our social conduct, else the storm of destruction and death will inevitably break upon us.

It is not a lack of patriotism or treason to make this revelation. It is because we know the law of cause and effect in the moral and political world, as in nature, that we warn America to-day. We know that the harvest of unbelief, of rationalism and pantheism, we are sowing in our institutions of learning will have to be reaped. Therefore, where is the true patriot who would not unite in the effort to bring about a reformation in all our sources of knowledge and education?

THE VALUE OF A TRUE EDUCATION

Our country has not as yet given sufficient attention to this question of education for the nation. We may imagine that for the government to suggest or advise or control in the matter of education in our higher institutions would be a violation of our freedom. But the government does this in our primary schools, high schools, normal schools, and state universities, and it is not an interference with our freedom. If the people should decide that certain philosophies and criticisms of the Word of God in our institutions are inimical to the political and religious well-being of the nation, then it is up to the people to make this one of the political questions and to elect men to represent them who will enact laws that shall regulate our institutions in regard to those anti-Christian philosophies and criticisms.

This is not a violation of our freedom, but an exercise of our right under the Constitution. In this we would be safe-guarding the future of America and of the world. Education is the most potent factor in the life of a nation for good or evil. The question that must be decided is, What shall be the character of our future education? It is not at the firesides of our farmers and tradesmen where revolution is born; it is the product of the teacher.

WHY NOT REGULATE OUR EDUCATIONAL INSTITUTIONS?

Our present universities, reeking with the unbelief of an evolutionistic false philosophy, are among the most dangerous centers in America. Educated young men have entered our universities to come out radical, anarchistic-socialists and agitators, agnostics, and haters of Christianity. And this also is the result, in some cases to-day of a theological training where the false philosophies and the result of the radical criticism are made the foundation of a system of theology.

Our Government has undertaken to regulate business, but the hour has come to regulate our higher education. Have not the people a right to say what shall be the type of men who shall teach in our schools, and what shall be the character of the sciences and philosophies that shall be studied? We protect our homes from the

vicious and criminal, and our food from adultera-
tions, and shall we not protect our young men and
women, in our institutions of learning, from the
breed of unregenerate infidels whose chief business in our high schools, normal schools, and
universities, seems to be to glorify a colossal
scientific or philosophical falsehood, and to
repudiate the only source of our highest wisdom
and knowledge, the Word of God? We jail the
poor soul who steals a loaf of bread; but the
teachers who steal from the rising generations
the bread of life, who turn noble Christian characters into agnostics and atheists, we elect them
to high offices, shower them with degrees, make
them the honored guests at our banquets, appoint
them the Presidents of universities, or send them
to Congress.

SHOULD BE TRUE TO OURSELVES

We should agitate and educate and arouse
America because we must in order to be true to
ourselves. If we know the Truth we should teach
it to others. If we know that war is the result
of a false education, a false philosophy of life,
that revolution is the fruit of rejection of Jesus
Christ as Master and Lord, then we must make
this fact known. Who is there that does not know
the secret of the greatness of the United States
and Great Britain? Devotion to the Sacred Word
is the only explanation of our high sense of justice,
our humanitarian activities. This is why America

and Britain are the masters of the world. God has given them this high place of trust and power because of their loyalty to His Laws. But shall it last?

A LESSON BY CONTRAST

We would do well to look at this great matter by way of contrast. We ask: What is Prussianism? Prussianism is a doctrine. It is a spirit also, but its spirit is the fruit of a doctrine. What is that doctrine? It is the opposite of Christianity. It is the doctrine that man is his own master, that the greatest thing is physical and intellectual force, that man is an evolved animal, that he cannot fall, and has never fallen, that he is always advancing, that he is his own saviour, and that the strong must rule, the weak perish. In brief, it is the rationalistic and evolutionistic doctrine that rejects the Bible as authority. This is Prussianism. And our American universities are the fostering hot-houses of this anti-Christian teaching, and some of the divinity schools add to this paganism the dignity and weight of their influence.

CHRISTIANITY DEFINED

On the other hand, Christianity is also a doctrine, but it is more, it is a life, it is a spirit, and its spirit is the product of its doctrine. Men talk against doctrine. If the doctrine of Christianity be omitted, there remains nothing of Christianity to preach or teach. Teaching Christianity without doctrine is like standing in the branches of a tree and sawing off the trunk beneath. Christianity without doctrine degenerates into an ethical anæmic. Doctrine means power. Doctrine is a mighty thing. The world is ruled by doctrine. Prussianism, a false doctrine, built on philosophy and science, has become entrenched in our institutions of learning. It rules out God— the personal loving God, it rules out Jesus Christ —the redeeming sacrificing Christ, it rules out the Bible, it enthrones man, it worships man, it glorifies force—physical force. And this is the doctrine taught more or less in many of our educational institutions to-day.

PRUSSIANISM OR CHRISTIANITY

Surely it is an easy matter to decide which of these two systems should hold sway in our education—Prussianism or Modernism, and Christianity?

What on the other hand is the Christian doctrine? We see it illustrated, in part, on the battlefields. A new world is appearing in Europe. Free nations are rising on the ruins of old autocracies and despotisms. The impulse of freedom is throbbing in the hearts of men. A world, while weeping over its dead, is singing its natal songs of a new political emancipation. The nations are being made free and safe for democracy. Glorious deliverance! Happy new birth! But for this redemption democracy had to pay the price. Our brave boys, and the brave boys of Britain, France, Canada, Australia, Japan, New Zealand, South Africa, Belgium, Serbia, Roumania, Greece, and India, had to pay the price of the world's liberation. Their dying groans and accents of praise still reverberate in our imagination and innermost chambers of our hearts. With smiles upon their transformed faces they bade adieu to loved ones. Even yet we think we hear them whisper in dying accents, "Farewell," " 'It is finished.' "

They knew that their blood was not given in vain, that the chains of autocracy would soon be broken, that they were dying for enemy as for friend, that nations might be free. This is the fact of substitution, and this fact of substitution is also the Christian doctrine, but carried into a still higher realm. It is the doctrine of the giving up of life for others that they may have an everlasting emancipation. "But we see Jesus Who was made a little lower than the angels for the suffering of death, crowned with glory and honor; that He by the grace of God should taste death for every man." (Heb. 2:9). "God so loved the world that He gave His only begotten Son that whosoever believeth on Him should not perish but have eternal life." (John 3:16). This is the great Christian doctrine. Our boys offered themselves up that nations might have a new birth of political freedom. Jesus Christ, God's Son, offered Himself up that the race might have

a new birth of spiritual freedom, eternal life—
that men everywhere might be delivered from the
kingdom of Satan, the slavery to the lower life,
and the curse of sin, and emancipated into the
glorious liberty of the sons of God—into the
higher Kingdom, the Kingdom of God. Men
admit the former, and weeping loved ones are
reconciled to it. They say with Caiaphas: "It is
expedient for us that one should die for the people
and that the whole nation perish not" (John
11:50). So we willingly gave our boys up to die
this substitutionary death that the whole world
might not politically perish. We gladly admit
this fact, and we are now entering into the joys
of our new political birth. Let us be as logical
and admit the Christian doctrine also. Jesus
Christ taught men how to die the substitutionary
death in loving service for others.

CHRISTIANITY DENIED

This then is the heart of the Christian doctrine.
And it is this, and the consequent new birth consciousness into the Kingdom of God, the higher
Kingdom, through the blood of Christ, that is
denied and ridiculed in our American institutions
by an imported paganism, which has substituted
in the place of the Christian doctrine, the theory
of evolution. It is this doctrine of Modernism
that robs man of his glory, and that presents the
greatest menace to the welfare of the world. If
we would keep America Christian and not

pagan, this false philosophy must be driven out
of our education, as it must also be driven out
of our pulpits, and the glorious old doctrine of
substitutionary and vicarious sacrifice and service
must take its place. The New Theology must go
if it means the destruction of some of our most
cherished notions. America must arise and drive
this enemy out. But first we must educate and
agitate. The public mind must be informed, the
conscience must be aroused. And it should be
made not only a religious question; it should
be discussed in our state legislatures and in Congress. It is a question also of national deliverance, and the nation should take up the task.

REFORMATION

We shall now advance and discuss, though not
following closely the order as given below, the
necessity for reformation in:

1. The theological seminary;
2. The lower schools and the universities;
3. The local churches.

Perhaps we should say revolution, for the
changes need be radical and fundamental affect-
ing the government of all these institutions. A
critic of the first edition of this book wrote: ''I
do not believe in fighting radicalism with radicalism.'' But when the changes necessary to be
effected are radical, then radicalism or moral
revolution is called for in dealing with the prob-

lem. In this sense the situation in many of our educational institutions calls for both reformation and moral revolution.

IN WHAT MUST THIS CHANGE CONSIST?

In a change of teachers, in some cases.

In a change of text-books and reference books used, in some cases.

In a change of trustees and managing boards, in some cases.

In a radical change in the methods of teaching. The use of the evolutionary hypothesis must be totally abandoned, except in the moral or spiritual realm. In this sphere there may be some ground for this hypothesis, but in every other realm it is an unproved and exceedingly harmful hypothesis.

The general custom of teaching a theory as a fact must be prohibited. The teacher must be taught to deal in a dogmatic way only with well known and established facts, and not deny the Scriptures that have been verified as historical and revealed truth by using a series of hypotheses —a sort of crazy quilt of unproved assumptions in the realm of science, philosophy and theology. And the teacher must learn to view man, not as an evolved animal, but as he is: a great moral spirit, made in the likeness of God, with an endless destiny. The dogmatist in the chair of science or philosophy must be taught to keep hands off God's Sacred Word.

OBLIGATION OF COLLEGE AND SEMINARY

It cannot reasonably be denied that our institutions furnish us with our greatest problem to-day; and it is difficult to tell whether the university or the theological seminary presents the most serious obstacle to Christianity. Probably the former, for not all our seminaries have gone over to Modernism. There are still a few in the Northern States that are loyal to God and His Truth and more in the South. But the college and the university, in nearly every case (the writer recalls only a few colleges in the North that are honorable exceptions) have been caught in the great delusion and are advocates of the anti-Christian doctrines. These great institutions are not doing the work for which they were founded and endowed. For instance, in the department of biology alone, is usually found a teacher who habitually states as a fact of evolution only that which is a mere conjecture, a poor lame theory. It need not be supposed that we are the enemy of our institutions because we seek for their improvement, and through these mighty agencies the highest welfare of our nation and the world.

INSTITUTIONS ARE TOO EXCLUSIVE

Our institutions are not intended to be exclusive and irresponsible concerns; they belong to the people, and the people have a right to call them to account, to demand that they give an account of their stewardship. Unfortunately, these institutions are too much of an irresponsible trust, or close autocratic organization, with a feeling of supreme independence and aloofness from the Christian churches. There should be some way devised to compel these institutions to give a full account of their work and teaching to some strong representative orthodox board, outside of their own boards and trustees. It is entirely too difficult a matter to-day to get a proper report from these institutions, and to get at, so to speak, those who are responsible as teachers for the modern religious demoralization. Because we are deeply dissatisfied, as stated, with the character of the work done by these institutions, it need not be taken as proof that we are their enemies. We are their truest friends, and it is because we are their friends, and desire for them the best, that we call upon the trustees and boards to bring about the needed changes, as already indicated.

TEACHER RULES THE WORLD

We do not view the work of the teacher in the high school, the college, and the university as we should. As a nation we have failed to understand the sacredness and seriousness of teaching the rising generations. Teaching is a high, a holy calling. The teacher is a creator and moulder of character. The teacher rules the world. His task is to build a great life, as well as to inform and train the intellect, and thus help fit men and women for both worlds, for his work, for good or ill, must have a direct and lasting bearing upon human destiny. But how can the teacher be qualified to do so great a work?

THE TEACHER'S EQUIPMENT

We know that infidelity, agnosticism, atheism, rationalism, and pantheism cannot equip the teacher for his calling. How can the teacher build a great life in the student if he does not teach the reality of the personal God, the glory of spiritual character, of the transforming power of Christian experience, under the leadership of Christ; and if he rejects the power and authority of the only Book that is capable of equipping the teacher to thus teach? America has been an orthodox, an evangelical country, the home of robust faith and glowing Christian love, until some decades ago when our universities began to flirt with German, British, and French rationalism and infidelity, and New England Unitarianism, since which time there has been a growing unrest, a religious deterioration, a marked downgrade movement, all of which began in the university. The teacher was then, as to-day, our problem, and our most responsible citizen.

LOVE AND WORSHIP OF CHRIST ESSENTIAL

We say it with a tremendous emphasis, that no one is qualified to teach our children who does not love Jesus Christ as Saviour and Lord, who does not strongly believe in the plenary inspiration of the Bible (by plenary we mean full, complete), who is not willing to give the Bible a higher and mightier place than it has ever had in our institutions, to recognize its power and greatness in the creation (not simply inspiration) of political and spiritual life, and to refer to it and teach it, not as he would refer to any other book, for there is no book of its kind. What is the Bible? It is not simply an illustration in history of the growth of religion; it speaks the final word to all the earth on this eternal theme. The Bible is not a book to jest about, laugh at, quibble over, belittle as authority on any subject. "It is the voice of Eternity to the hearts of men." Man cannot answer Eternity. Here in the presence of destiny science cannot speak, philosophy is dumb, but the Bible comes with a commanding, majestic, authoritative message of hope and assurance.

SURFACE TRIBUTE NOT ENOUGH

The work of the teacher, we repeat, should make this clear to the student. The usual courteous profession of external and traditional reverence for the Bible will not suffice. Such surface tribute and good manners we respect, but it is not enough. The teacher should feel it his duty and high privilege to refer to the Bible "as the record of the infallible Spirit of God, Who, in its sacred pages, struggles to speak to men."

He should be qualified to teach that the secret of the Bible is not higher criticism, lower criticism, textual criticism, destructive criticism, or any other kind of criticism, but a new creation; that this Book is the world's Book, humanity's Book; that it goes to the innermost of the world's conscience; that it is the charter of the world's destiny; and that it should be given its rightful place in the life of the student and in our educational institutions. Here we can put our finger on the cause of the unrest and strife and sorrow that has in recent times deluged our world—the Bible has not been given its rightful place in the world's education.

THE SITUATION IN THE SEMINARY

Let us look at the problem as found in our theological schools. Here, where the Bible should be supreme, absolute, it must in most classes take a secondary place to a certain philosophy of interpretation of history, the philosophy of evolution. Like in the university, philosophy and science are the great authorities. This accounts for the fact that a theological training to-day, in many cases, is really more of a hindrance than a help to the work of preaching the Gospel. Romanism locks the Bible up, or forbids their people reading it, except under certain conditions. The Greek church of Russia does likewise. But in Germany, Britain and America—the great Protestant nations, made strong by a reverent study of the Bible in past centuries—we are, in our institutions in these countries, reading the Bible, but, as result of a false philosophy, it is viewed as of secondary value. It is interpreted and studied very much as Shakespeare or Emerson is studied—as a human product only. Thus the Bible is stripped of its power and glory.

CATHOLICS AND THE BIBLE

As to the attitude of the Roman Catholic Church toward the Bible, and the attitude of our American universities, our preference would be the former, though we deplore both. In the Roman church the Bible is gagged, that is, it is not permitted to speak, lest it lessen the authority of the hierarchy.

AN UNKNOWN TONGUE

In the university, however, it is made to speak, but in an unknown tongue. This fact explains why some young men were, as preachers, more acceptable before they entered the seminary than after their graduation. In some cases the graduates go out into the world not knowing just what to believe or preach.

The churches gave their noblest young men to the seminary, with their prayers, their love, their gifts; but what in some cases does the seminary give back? Not the young man with the same strong faith and glowing love. True, he has a trained intellect, but he is uncertain as to the essentials. He is now unstable in his opinions. He is a semi-radical critic, or possibly full-fledged, a sort of polite and diplomatic doubter of the great facts which he formerly held as fundamental in Christianity. Is this type of young preacher an improvement on his former self, or is he one of the tragedies of the twentieth century?

THE TRUE WORK OF THE SEMINARY:

And this brings us face to face with the query, What is the purpose of a theological seminary? We answer, To train young men to understand the divine-human art of advancing the Church and Kingdom of God. Jesus tells us how the Kingdom is advanced. He says that the good seed are the children of the Kingdom; and again he says that the Word of God is the Kingdom seed, and from sowing both the Kingdom advances—grows. This is the material the Spirit of God always uses. Now this makes plain the work of a theological seminary, which is to interpret and implant the Word of God in the student's heart, and to teach him how to do likewise, namely: to properly interpret and implant the Word in the hearts of men by the art of preaching; and also to make clear to the student that he is called to give up every ounce of his life in holy, loving, sacrificial service for the advancement or growth of the Church and Kingdom of God.

MANUFACTURING DOUBTERS

It stands to reason that if the seminary manufactures doubters instead of men of great faith, it is not doing its legitimate work. A doubter is a menace to the Church and never a sign of growth or religious health. Our Lord made it plain that doubt is the most powerful obstacle to the progress of His Church. His challenge to men is always the challenge to faith. Hear Him: "If thou canst believe." "These signs shall follow them which believe." "O fools, and slow of heart, to believe all that the prophets have spoken." "The devil taketh away the Word, lest they believe." The Apostle Paul presents this deadly disease of doubt in this fashion: "He that doubteth is damned . . . for whatsoever is not of faith is sin." One of the great things about the prophet Daniel that attracted King Belshazzar to him was, that he was a "dissolver of doubts." Even this heathen King had some knowledge of the value of Daniel's faith in the living God. Perhaps the greatest thing in a preacher's life is faith, in fact, in any life. The seminary is the institution where doubt should perish. Every teacher in this sacred and honored school should, by his life, but especially by his true interpretation of the Bible, exert such an influence that doubt must die in his presence. If the student enters the seminary in a state of mental uncertainty as to any of the great facts of the

Bible, it is the imperative business of the seminary to remove, by its safe and sane and true spiritual teaching of the Sacred Word, all doubt, and strongly establish the student in his faith in the Bible, as the veritable Word of God to men. If the seminary fails here it fails everywhere, but alas (we say it with a pain in the heart) here is where the seminary often fails.

THE SEMINARY OBJECTS

It may be objected that the students bear testimony to the helpfulness of the seminary course to them, and that they leave the institution strong in faith. Possibly this is true of some. But we must not judge the students so much by their own testimony as by their after ministry and its results. The atmosphere of doubt created in the New Theology class-room must make its mark upon even those students who did not accept this point of view of the Bible, though they themselves are unaware of it. No Christian can come under such teaching for three years and not be influenced more or less. We grant that some noble men graduate from our seminaries, and go out to do a great work, but it is not due to any help they received from the New Theology, but rather in spite of that teaching, and is the result of the teaching of the good Old Theology of the Incarnation, of Calvary, and the Open Grave. In most seminaries in the North one teacher in four is an advocate of Modernism, but that is one-fourth too many. It matters not how enthusiastic the student may appear to be over this teaching, we must judge him by his ministry. The teaching that kills the spirit of prayer in a church, and often alienates some of the most intelligent Bible students, cannot be of God.

NEW THEOLOGY MEN FAIL

It is true that Old Theology preachers sometimes fail to make good, for some men mistake their calling, but their failure was not the result of their theology. Some are preaching orthodoxy and heterodoxy, New and Old Theology, who ought to be in other service. But when we recall four preachers who were able ministers of the Gospel when they entered the seminary, but who while there adopted the New Theology, and failed as a result thereof, then we know for a certainty that the New Theology is a menace to the Church of God. One of these preachers is now making coffins, another tombstones, another is an undertaker, while the fourth is now a rabid socialistic agitator, denouncing the Bible and Christianity.

MUST NOT BLAME THE STUDENTS

Furthermore, the blame for this must not be put on the character of the men whom the churches send to the seminary. The seminary teacher was only partly right, in his reply to the church that complained of the type of men he had sent to

them, when he said: "If you will send us better
material, we will send you better ministers." The
divinity students are, as a class, a fair average
physically, mentally and spiritually, and have in
them the possibilities, if properly trained, of the
making of useful ministers of Jesus Christ. Our
problem lies not in the kind of men who enter the
modern New Theology seminary, but in the type
of men who come out. If the Truth were fully
taught, the student would graduate, to go out into
the world a living flame.

A FALSE EMPHASIS

The New Theology teacher develops the brain
but not the heart, but God is looking for men
bigger in heart than in head, mightier in love than
in cold intellectual criticism. For example, if the
student enters the seminary lacking the ability to
conduct, let us say, a small spiritual revival in
a modest church, the seminary ought to so develop
his heart, enrich his spiritual life, that the result
in his ministry would naturally be a healthy and
continuous revival of pure religion. Our great
problem to-day is that, in not a few cases, the
students enter as evangelists, or fairly capable
Gospel preachers, and while in the seminary lose
this glowing passion which is born of the Spirit
and Truth of God. Surely the Bible is not to
blame for this loss of power while in the seminary.

As someone has well said: "The Bible belongs
to the literature of power," and a seminary

course should teach the student to draw on that power, to put himself back into the great spiritual atmosphere of the Bible. "The speech of the Bible is the speech of the heart, and it must be read with the heart."

The New Testament and the Old are God's great heart-throb expressed through men, giving them a great experience; consequently, experience is the key to its meaning.

This, however, the New Theology critic does not understand. He comes to the Bible with his cold scientific theories, and his critical faculties all on edge, and studies it before his class very much as a surgeon performs an operation, as if he were looking for some sore or diseased part or ailment of some kind.

THE PROFESSOR'S COUNSEL

As a teacher of Modernism recently said to his students in the writer's presence: "As we approach the study of this Book of Revelation, we are not supposed to take anything for granted. We must not even assume that this Book belongs to the Sacred Canon." It looked very much as if the Bible were put on trial for its life, like a prisoner in court. But the Bible is not on trial, it is the New Theology critic who is on trial. The schools cannot finally judge the Bible, by the Bible we must judge the schools. The New Theology does not give the Bible a real chance in the classroom to answer back and defend itself.

HOW THE SEMINARY CAN TEACH THE BIBLE

But this scientific and critical method is false. By it we can never judge or know our Bible. "The only commentary on the Bible of any value is Christian struggle, experience and prayer," that alone puts the student in the Bible atmosphere and teaches him the Bible tongue. To know the Bible, therefore, we must first know its Heavenly Author. "We grant the Bible is to be understood, but it also is to be enjoyed." Its rich treasure of Truth cannot be discovered by the so-called scientific method. One day of prayerful meditation over the Bible is more successful as a method of study than one year of critical analysis.

SPIRITUAL CULTURE SUPREME

Let the seminary teachers abandon this critical method, as of paramount importance, and turn their great institution into more of a center of prayer and deeply spiritual culture, more of a holy retreat, where the student will feel that this is a holy place, to him the very gate of Heaven; and a place where graduates in after years will be glad to gather as to a refreshing oasis in life's desert for reinforcement for new struggles. Seasons of prolonged prayer with fasting should, at least, be taught as imperative, if not made a part of a seminary course. Let the seminary specialize in spiritual religion, and burn their text-books on higher, or more properly called, radical criticism, and New Theology, and see what God will do for this sacred school of the prophets. We unhesitatingly declare, that if this were done, the modern seminary would soon become the fountain-head of glorious revivals of religion—a river of blessing to the thirsty world. But shall the student study? Yes, verily; but let an exalted type of religion come first! Let the theological seminary be turned into a sacred altar where God loves to meet His servants and reveal to them His will and baptize them with His power.

THE PROBLEM COMPLICATED

Well-meaning teachers have tried to justify their methods of teaching, especially the so-called scientific and critical or historical method. Much time in this sort of study has been justified on the ground that the student needs to be fortified and made acquainted with the most destructive criticism (both with its methods and result) and with those objections to what the critic is pleased to term, the "weak parts" of the Bible, in order to know how to meet them. This apology for the destructive critical study was frequently advanced when the writer was in the seminary. But after twenty odd years of experience and study, as we view the situation to-day, all such defense of a false criticism seems absurd, as if the spiritual realities of the Bible need any such support. As well defend breathing and the shining of the sun as defend in this sort of a stupid fashion the Word of Almighty God.

THE SEMINARY APOLOGY

But the seminary tells us that the New Theology type of thinker is needed in order that the student may know all sides of these great questions. They say that to-day the students from the universities come to the seminary unsettled in faith, and that the New Theology doctors are necessary to treat their ailments. This recalls a recent correspondence between the Dean of one of our best known seminaries and a thoughtful layman, an officer in a local church, over this very matter.

CORRESPONDENCE BETWEEN DEACON AND DEAN

The writer was furnished with a copy of this correspondence by the courtesy of the deacon, and the portion is herewith submitted that bears directly upon the question we are now discussing. About a half dozen letters or more had already been exchanged in which the Dean declared his belief in the orthodox views of his own Denomination. The church of which this officer is a member sent to the seminary their annual offering, but this time with an accompanying protest against the New Theology in that institution.

This was what started the extended correspondence.   While the Dean declared himself as orthodox, yet strange to say, he comes to the defense of the teacher in theology, who is an advocate of Modernism, and tries to justify his presence and work in the seminary.

He says in part:

THE DEAN'S LETTER:

I did not answer the last letter . . . because the matter does not lie in my jurisdiction.   [The Dean here refers to a question put to him in a former letter, in which he was asked why, since he claims to be orthodox, he supports Dr. C.—we will call him Dr. C., the professor in theology who does not believe or teach the orthodox views, or words to that effect.]   While I am Dean, I am at the same time only a member of the faculty with no power of appointing or dismissing professors.

But I should like to say a word with reference to Dr. C. continues the Dean.   I know he is assailed from many sides, and I am frank to say that he and I do not agree in our opinions. [Note carefully the Dean does not believe in Dr. C.'s opinions.] At the same time I recognize the value of the service he is rendering.

The Dean continues:

Let me try to make clear what it is.   I wonder if you have children of your own in high school.   If so, perhaps you have had my experience.   My boy came home to tell me that he did not believe the Bible.   Why?   Because the teaching he got in the school with reference to the creation of the world he could not square with Genesis.   So far as I am aware, the theory which he was given is generally taught and lots of our high-school boys and girls are in trouble.   The whole matter is intensified in college where the course in science and philosophy seems so contradictory to the conceptions that our young men and women have held that they become greatly unsettled.   That is not true merely of this college or that, but of practically all our colleges. I do not mean to imply that the introduction to the marvels of the universe as science presents them opens a new world to our young people in which they often have difficulty in adjusting themselves.

I suggest this much to let you see something of the problem we face in the seminary. Our young people are unsettled when they come to us, and it makes little difference from what college they have come. It is our business to help them, to try to relate their thinking in the realm of religion to their thinking in other realms, to make them see that the God of the universe is one and that rightly understood there can be no contradiction between His revelation in nature and His revelation in the Scripture. I assure you that the task is not an easy one, and its nature and demands are constantly changing. But we must get our young men through to something positive, else they will have no message. . . .

That particular thing Dr. C., as I have learned from the testimony of many young men, seems to be able to accomplish. I know that our college men go to him with their problems and get help. I assure you he helps many young men into settled convictions. He is not a destroyer of the faith of men.[1]

After a few more words of eulogy of Dr. C., whose opinions the Dean himself says he does not accept, he concludes with these words:

I am glad also to cherish the confidence that our graduates give proof in their ministry of the soundness of their faith.

ANALYSIS OF LETTER:

A number of things stand out prominent in this remarkable letter:

1. The Dean does not agree with the opinions of the professor in theology, Dr. C.

---

[1] Since the Dean wrote the above letter the professor in theology, Dr. C. has been dismissed for teaching heresy, or Modernism.

2. There is a teaching in high school and university antagonistic to the Bible that unsettles our young people, and that the students enter the seminary to-day in this unsettled state of mind.

3. The New Theology professor Dr. C., who does not believe in the inspiration of the Bible is the expert in this seminary in the business of doctoring the religious ailments of these incoming students.

4. The graduates give proof in their ministry of the soundness of their faith.

Before discussing this diagnosis of the seminary problem from the standpoint set forth in the Dean's letter, we submit the reply by the officer of the local church. Let us call him deacon A.

THE DEACON'S LETTER:

Deacon A says:

I am glad to note by yours of . . . that you do not agree with Dr. C., the professor in theology.

Regarding the fourth paragraph of your letter, I have children in school. Whenever my children have come to me with doubts about the validity of the statements in the Bible, because the same were in supposed conflict with science, I have taken the necessary time to prove to them that in times past, whenever there were differences, it was the scientists' that were in error, and that the statements of the Word of God were absolute, and this being true, they should side with the Bible whenever its statements were contradicted by scientists.

As to the next paragraph of your letter: I agree with the thought expressed therein, but I do not believe that you are doing what you are trying to do, nor do I believe that you can do it so long as you have the teaching which is destructive to unqualified belief in the Word of God.

Regarding the last paragraph in your letter, I wish to, in the most kindly way possible, undeceive you in the confidence you have in your graduates. For a long time I was a member of a church whose pastor was one of your graduates, and I have heard many other graduates of your institution preach in many towns and cities, and I have had many personal talks with them. The pastor of my church, referred to above, prided himself on being able to (quoting from the third paragraph, second page of your letter) "give much needed help at a critical time to many young people" and that was true, although it was equally true that his teaching was so contrary to the truth as expressed in the Scriptures as to cause some to leave the church and go where they could find the *Truth*.

My talks with the other graduates, also students of your seminary, all go to make me believe that the destructive criticism taught by Professor C. is most destructive to the faith of the students and that those who really absorb his teachings are the worse for having done so.

To this able letter the Dean made no reply. This correspondence confirms the truth as stated in these pages, namely: that there is a momentous conflict to-day in our institutions over the Bible, and that undoubtedly the faith of many is being shattered.

THE SEMINARY IS PLAYING FAST AND LOOSE

But to come back to the Dean's letter. Here we find the head of a great theological institution professing to believe in the orthodox doctrines of Christianity and that he does not agree with the New Theology of Dr. C., yet supporting Dr. C., in his views and work in the seminary. What shall we call this? Camouflage, politics, dishonest hedging? There is a serious implication in the Dean's words which, to say the least, does not reflect favorably upon his own views or ability, and also the other members of the faculty. It is only to the New Theology doctor that the young people go in his seminary for help in their problems. Of course the Dean does not mean to thus discredit himself or his colleagues. Would it seem that what the Dean meant to do was to defend the teaching of the New Theology in his seminary, and, by way of implication, discredit the good Old Theology which he professed to believe? Would it appear that his professed allegiance to the old doctrines is not to be taken seriously? The Standard Dictionary defines hypocrisy as: "feigning to be what one is not; insincerity." Shall we dare imagine that the Dean of the theological seminary is a hypocrite? In charity we must not judge.

THE DEAN'S TESTIMONY AS TO OTHER SCHOOLS

The Dean affirms that the high schools and universities unsettle the faith of their students in the Bible. It would be interesting to know how many of our students in these institutions who feel called to the ministry are turned aside to other service because of the anti-Christian teaching. It is probably true that in this fact we have

one of the principal causes of the decline in the
number of students in our seminaries in recent
years. The Church should, without delay, be apprised of the fact that much of our education is
anti-Bible, anti-Christian. Probably this explains
in part the decline in church attendance in
America. The foundation of the Church is being
gradually undermined in our secular institutions
of learning. The great question is, how long will
the Church be able to endure this serious assault,
this underhanded, indirect, or treacherous blow
in the back, by those institutions which exist
largely on her generosity, her self-sacrificing support? Shall the Church continue to ignore this
momentous matter, or shall the forces of
Evangelical Christianity in America rise up and
remedy this evil? The Church alone must answer
this question. The Dean of the seminary has
done some good service in pointing out the fact
afresh that the character of the teachings in high
school and university creates a serious problem
for the seminary. But to come back to the
seminary.

NO REMEDY IN THE NEW THEOLOGY

The New Theology which creates doubt as to
the inspiration of the Bible has no real remedy
for the perplexed student. The highest science is
the knowledge of Jesus Christ. But the system
that weakens the faith of the student in the only
Book that tells us about Jesus Christ is neither

scientific nor Christian. It is absurd to suppose, as teachers sometimes do, that it is not scientific to be orthodox. "The Modernist rails against the dogmatism of the orthodox, yet he himself is so dogmatic and authoritative as to give orthodoxy no quarter whatever."

The thing we need to know beyond a doubt is, that there is no conflict between the Truth, there is conflict only between Truth and error, the Kingdom of God and the kingdom of Satan.. God is in harmony with Himself in the natural as in the spiritual world. There is no conflict, therefore, between our Lord Jesus Christ and the Bible on one hand, and science and philosophy on the other hand. If there appears to be a contradiction here, it must be between false interpretations of the Bible and the immature or false conclusions of science, or between what we may call the religionist and the scientist. The reason for the unsettlement of our students in high schools and universities is that they are not taught this fact.

HOW TO REMOVE DOUBT

But it requires two sets of powers or faculties in men to interpret God's Truth, or the facts of nature and the Truth of Holy Scripture, namely: the natural faculties, or the intellect, and the spiritual faculties, the principal organ of which is faith. Only the man of faith can understand spiritual realities. A man may be a scholar and capable of teaching in any university, but if he has not learned to study the Bible in a reverent, childlike faith, he can not possibly learn the secret of this great Book. Prayer cannot, for instance, be studied in the laboratory, and neither can the theory of biological and geological and psychological evolution be properly used as a principle of interpretation of the Bible. The Bible will not yield its treasure to any such application. As the Apostle Paul says: "Man by wisdom," that is by scholarship, "knows not God."

If the teachers in the seminaries would make these facts plain to the unsettled students coming from other schools, they would quickly and easily solve their problems. A man may be ignorant in the knowledge of books and a master scientist in the knowledge of God and His Truth. And the opposite is true, namely: a man may be a great scholar, but if he has not an experimental knowledge of God, he cannot possibly know or interpret the Bible. Scholarship, therefore, without Jesus Christ in the heart, who is the revelation of the Father, and of the heart of the Bible as well, is foolishness with God. The so-called scientific method, as we have already stated, cannot possibly interpret the Bible. The best doctor for the perplexed spirit of man is not the New Theology critic, but the Great Physician who made the soul. Let the student learn this fact and soon he will become proficient in the science of God—he will learn the secret of the Bible.

WHY THE BIBLE TRAINING SCHOOLS ARE GROWING

In the light of what has been said, we can see the cause of the popularity of the rapidly growing Bible Training Schools in America, and the decline in what ought to be a still greater institution, the theological seminary. This is the only possible explanation of the success of the former —they give the Word of God its true place, they permit it to do its own work unhindered by any quasi-theory of historical or critical science, or of evolution. And the Bible, if permitted, is fully capable of doing its own appointed work. This is why not a few of our perplexed students from the universities, who take a course in our Bible Training Schools, graduate as flaming evangelists, or consecrated Christian workers in other callings.

THE SEMINARY SHOULD BE OUR GREATEST INSTITUTION

We would say it in all humility, let the theological seminaries learn wisdom and change their methods, and renounce their historical criticism, and New Theology point of view. We are laboring for this great reform in our institutions because we desire the Church to gain and not suffer a continuous loss. We have this splendid property, these magnificent buildings, and the prestige of a glorious history. Shall we not, then, men and women of the Christian Churches, demand, in the spirit of kindness and good will, a change, and thus bring about in the truest, the highest sense, the permanent deliverance of these great institutions?

The theological seminary has been the greatest asset the churches have had in the past, and with wise and consecrated management, these institutions would continue to be in the future still larger channels of blessing. Surely, as result of the study of all these facts, the reader must have arrived at the conclusion that the New Theology of Modernism must be separated from our institutions of learning.

CHAPTER VIII

THE REMEDY—REFORMATION BY THE CHURCHES

It will be the local churches that will bring to pass the much needed reforms in our institutions, and within their own Denominations.

Every upward movement in history has had its inspiration and origin in the Church of God, not necessarily in the hierarchy or ecclesiastical side of the Church, but in the great ecclesia, the called out, Spirit-baptized Body of Jesus Christ, or the true Church of God.

PURITAN NEW ENGLAND AND SLAVERY

It was the Puritan spirit of New England that kindled the flame of indignation against slavery in this nation, that finally resulted in its destruction. The New York Globe has recently said that, to the Baptist, Presbyterian, and Methodist Bodies in America, belong the credit for the partial, and what will ultimately prove to be the complete destruction of the liquor traffic. Some of the prelates of the Catholic Church defended the great abomination, the liquor traffic; but in this deplorable conduct, these men were not quite in line with "apostolic succession," as were the

216

democratic, Evangelical, Protestant Bodies. The true spiritual Church has in every country been the salt of society and the light of the world. It was this true Church as seen in prophecy—(the men and women of faith in God and loyalty to his Truth)—of which God spoke when He said to Abraham: "And in thee shall all families of the earth be blessed" (Gen. 12:3).

PROTESTANTISM WON THE WAR

In the terrible war now gloriously won, who have been the guiding spirits, the men of wide vision, of heroic leadership? They are nearly all the sons of Protestant Churches.

Lloyd George, the Welsh Baptist; Mr. Balfour, the Anglican; Premier Borden, of Canada, the Nova Scotia Presbyterian; Theodore Roosevelt, of the Reformed Church; Woodrow Wilson, Presbyterian; General Foch, a Roman Catholic, but a man of a liberal Protestant mind and spiritual experience.

These were the great souls, who, with many others, led the world out of its despair by bringing to pass the destruction of Prussian militarism. For this mighty service the whole world is indebted to the Christian Church. It was Protestantism that saved the world for democracy, and that must save democracy for the world. It was the descendants of the Puritans and the Pilgrim Fathers, the children of Luther, Latimer, Ridley,

Calvin, Knox, Bunyan, Wesley, that comprised seventy-five per cent. of the British and American armies; that sprung to the rescue of France and Belgium and Italy and other oppressed peoples, and, with the heroes of those great nations, won the victory. Of course we would not disparage the work done by Roman Catholics. But it was Protestantism, Christian Protestantism, with its lofty national ideals, and under the leadership of Jesus Christ, that has delivered the world. And there is resident in our Protestant Churches the possibilities of all kinds of helpful reform.

THE CHURCHES CAN WIN

The solution of our present problem will have to be found in these same spiritual forces. The genius of Protestantism is that it can reform itself from within, and direct the destinies of the nations from without. Its spiritual baptism is the secret of its moral illumination, its ethical vitality and power. We shall enumerate some things which the churches can and ought to do.

THE CHURCHES CAN PROTEST

The churches can make a strong protest against the New Theology teaching, in all our institutions. This is our first and most imperative duty. We can at least protest. As the late Rev. Edward Judson of New York once said: "A Protestant ought to have, at least, a protest in him."

The writer knows of one church in New York State that has recently made this protest against the teachings in one of our divinity schools. This was done on the occasion of sending the annual offering to the Education Society of this Denomination. This church debated whether they should longer support the said Society, but finally decided to send the offering with their protest against the teaching in the seminary; and that, doubtless, made an impression, as it created a lengthy correspondence regarding the work done in this institution. Part of this correspondence we incorporated in our previous chapter.

A NOTE OF PROTEST

DEAR SIR:

Doubtless you have been somewhat surprised at not receiving an earlier reply to your letter concerning our Easter offering. Am sorry to say it was only after considerable discussion that it was decided to send you this offering. We understand, however, that certain things are being taught at both [mentioning two seminaries in New York State], which are not in harmony with the principles or beliefs of our Denomination. It was finally voted to send you the offering, with our *protest* against the teaching of this so-called "new thought."

This was wise and timely service. Of course it takes some courage to make a protest of this kind, but where is there the church that has not the Christian manhood to do it? This at least should be done. Of course some will object. Modernism has friends here and there in the churches, and some of these **are** prominent in the official boards; but this opposition can be overcome. If it should appear too strong for victory in the official board, let the pastor or some active layman bring the matter before a meeting of the entire church, after mature thought and careful preparation. Remember that everything worth while in this world has had to encounter opposition. Prejudice, pride, and ignorance often play a large part in all unworthy opposition to noble causes. One of the things that Zechariah saw in his vision was "Joshua the high priest standing before the Angel of the Lord and Satan standing by his right hand" (Zechariah 3:1). There is where Satan stands. He is present at every service in the church, and stands, the invisible devil, by the side of every true preacher in the pulpit, and saint in the pew. But let not the church hesitate, let her be strong and courageous, and not undervalue this splendid service. The old adage is so true—"A stitch in time saves nine," and a simple protest by the churches sent to our various institutions may be the means of heading off what might ultimately prove to be the destruction of our civilization. This is a most valuable, a momentous thing to do, and let the churches resort without delay to this method and take the first step in our great reform. If the church, as a body, should be defeated in this, then let some society in the church send its protest!

PRACTICAL INSTRUCTIONS

Notice of such action should be sent to the officers of the institution or institutions, a copy to the president, one to the secretary, and one to the treasurer of the managing boards, and trustees, with a copy forwarded to the Denominational paper or papers for publication. The action of each church would thus be an incentive to others to follow their lofty example.

In churches, whose pulpits are enslaved by the New Theology, let wise, brave men secure a protest there also against the teaching in our institutions. This would also serve as a powerful warning to the deluded man in the pulpit, to get back to the gospel of Christ. These churches ought to be good judges of Modernism, as they have first-hand knowledge of it, if by it they have not been blinded to the Truth. Some churches have seen the New Theology alienate some of its noblest members from their fellowship. These members went away in order to protest in this way against this false system; let the churches profit by their example, and rise up and do their duty. Let them show their concern for sister churches, and their love for the brethren. Many of the great laws passed in Congress in recent years were put through because millions of voters registered by letter to their representatives their approval of these laws, while similarly vicious measures were defeated by the same method. Let the churches everywhere protest.

INDIVIDUALS SHOULD PROTEST

Furthermore, let individuals also protest as individuals. Many thousands of persons are contributors to these institutions, let them register their hearty disapproval. Let them serve notice that they will withhold their gifts until the desired reforms are brought to pass. *Money talks.*

IS A BOYCOTT JUSTIFIABLE?

This raises the question of boycott by the orthodox forces. Should we withhold our donations as churches and individuals from our colleges, universities, seminaries, and other schools where Modernism is taught? This in nearly every case would surely be a wise thing to do. Paul said: "If meat make my brother to offend I will eat no flesh while the world standeth." (I Cor. 8:13). Magnificent! Could not Christians rightly say in the light of this principle, or better ought they not to say: If contributing to these institutions causes them to continue feeling secure and safe in their unscriptural teaching, and thus leading astray our young men and women for whom Christ died, I will give them no further gifts, no not so long as the world standeth, or at any rate so long as they continue to teach the rationalistic philosophies and the New Theology. When they dismiss all such teachers and abandon their text-books and reference books then I shall give them a hearty support.

A CHASTISEMENT OF LOVE

It is believed that this would be a proper and wise chastisement of the institutions we love. Indeed, this sort of conduct by churches and individuals would be a proof of our love and deep interest in their highest welfare. Giving to these institutions as at present conducted may be heaping fuel upon a flame that is destined ultimately to destroy our churches. We know what New England Unitarianism has done for New England, how it has turned the people by thousands away from the churches; and by this we may know what an intensified Unitarian propaganda would do for America and the world, for this is, in part, what the New Theology movement is in the realm of education.

If the financial support of these institutions by the churches is continued for a decade or two longer they will become so heavily endowed that action of the above sort would have no effect upon them. In fact this, unfortunately, is already the case with some of them. They have been endowed by good meaning noble men and women, and the false teacher feels comfortable and secure therein.

PROTECTION OF LOCAL CHURCH

There is another service the local churches can render: They can guard their pulpits at home against every teacher and preacher of Modern-

ism. Not only should the Christian people withhold their sons and their daughters and their gifts
from those schools where the New Theology is
taught, but they should bar their pulpits at home
against these subtle deceivers no matter how winning their personality and brilliant their gifts.
If the churches cannot secure safe and sane and
sound ministers for their pulpits from the regular
seminaries, let them call upon the Practical Bible
Training Schools for ministers to teach and lead
them.   These schools have become strong and
noted for the splendid character of their work,
and no church need hesitate to welcome their
students to their pulpits.   There are to be found
in these schools, to-day, some of the ablest and
most helpful Bible teachers in the world.   There
are still, however, a few theological seminaries
where only the grand old doctrines are taught.
*The churches should support these, and seek
through them men to serve as pastors, for these
are our most valuable religious schools.*

But after the candidate for the pulpit has been
heard, or if possible, better still, before he is
heard to preach, let him be thoroughly examined
as to his views regarding the Incarnation, the
Atonement of Christ, the Resurrection of the
body, and the Second Coming of Christ in personal and bodily appearance.   If he is sound on
these great doctrines of Revelation he is sound
everywhere.

PULPIT BARRED TO NEW THEOLOGY

Not, however, under any circumstances should the New Theology advocates have an opportunity to preach, for these are cunning men, they are adepts at feigning orthodoxy, and hiding their real views, in order to get a call, and after they get a call, in order to hold a pastorate, their destructive teaching will be dealt out stealthily, in small doses, gentle subtle hints, and suggestions, until they have won the congregation, after which it is no easy matter to get rid of the destroyer of the true Faith, of the enemy of the blood of Christ, and His Glorious Appearing.

DISMISSING NEW THEOLOGY PREACHER

If the New Theology preacher is in the pulpit what shall the church do? Shall he be retained or dismissed? He has made friends, secured a following, and not a few ill-informed persons in the Word of God think he is doing a good work. He is pleasant, affable in manner and talented in speech. Dismissing him might rupture the church. What shall be done? The answer is, dismiss him even at the cost of a disruption. It is better to divide the church in a righteous effort to get rid of the false teacher in the pulpit than it is to have the real work of the church nullified— that is, as an evangelical, upbuilding, and soul-winning institution. If the New Theology teacher remains it is only a matter of time when the church will go over to this Unitarian propaganda. It is better to save half or part of the church than none at all. The New Theology teaching in an orthodox church is like a foul stream running into a pure stream, the latter will soon become foul. The insidious work will be going on silently, and the church will soon become, unconsciously, a victim of the delusion.

THE HOUR HAS COME

Surely the hour has come when the men and women of the churches should grapple with this momentous matter. The enemy of the Cross has already become entrenched within our gates, and not a few of the churches are being slowly won away from the Lord who bought them. They are directing their attack against the whole line of Christian doctrine. Now they deny the inspiration of the Bible, then the Deity of our Lord, again Christian baptism, then the new birth, and the Second Coming of our Lord, then they say we are "narrow-minded sectarian bigots," and so on, until by their cunning subtle teaching they have undermined the whole system of Revelation.

We make our appeal to the sane men and women of the churches, and to the official boards in all our institutions. It is within the power of the churches to solve this problem. Shall we do it? We appeal to the local churches to withhold their gifts from every teacher of Modernism. This is not the day for time-serving in pulpit or pew. Christianity in America and the world is facing a crisis from which the smoothness of underhanded diplomacy and flattery cannot save us. Let us as with one voice declare that the New Theology must go from our pulpits and institutions of learning. If we fail now, our churches, as evangelical institutions, must disintegrate and perish from the earth. If our gifts, our support is not withheld now from this Christless propaganda, and our hands and hearts cleansed from giving any sort of co-operation to these deluded men who would undermine the foundation laid in the blood of Christ for the upbuilding of the Kingdom of God, then we are unworthy children of the Pilgrim Fathers, of the Puritans, of the Reformers, of the mighty host that gave up their lives for these great things for which we should strive and live. Let the blood of the martyrs speak to us to-day! If we prove true to our trust, and pass on to our children the priceless legacy of God's eternal Truth, then heaven will crown the service, a great new day of life will dawn for the churches, streams of salvation will flow in our midst, times of unbounded refreshing will be ours, and the wide world will reverberate with His praise. We would say in the words of the great Scotch Preacher, Dr. Chalmers, "What we most need is the expulsive power of a great affection." We have now the vision. God give the courage necessary to perform our holy task.

MUCH HELP IN REVIVALS

After all has been said, it should not be forgotten that the most fundamental need is for more sound teaching in our schools and a mighty outpouring of the Spirit of God. If the churches and the institutions could see this and seek for a great revival of religion, God could then clear away the rubbish that has clogged the streams of His grace and keep them flowing. But it must begin with the pulpit and the teacher, or it must reach these men in high places as well as the lowliest. How God could bring this to pass we do not know. It may be through a great national calamity like an earthquake, or a flood, or social revolution, or civil war. For this heavenly dynamic, a revival of pure religion, let us earnestly work and pray. With such religious awakening it would then be easier to proceed with the work of reform in our institutions. With a spiritual momentum back of the Christian forces they would move forward like a flood; but without this it must needs be an uphill pull.

It is earnestly believed that this is one of the causes of the departure from the Truth to-day—the lack of interest in the salvation of men, or in revivals of religion. The writer has never known a church to be led astray by the New Theology that was busy with its pastor, laboring for the salvation of souls. When this, the supreme mission of the Church in the world is forgotten, then it is natural to expect that heresy and schism will paralyze the professing body of Christ. "Our hope is in the God who made heaven and earth." We depend on Him. Let the reader get a fresh hold of Him and His promises in prayer. America must have a great national revival of religion, or Christianity as a vital spiritual reality will perish from this land. Doubtless, if we undertake to do the work outlined in these pages God will graciously reward us with the power and blessing we need.

THE RESTORED CHRIST

"There was a wealthy patron of art who greatly admired the Spanish painter Murillo. One day the rich man ran across a masterpiece of Murillo's—a representation of the infant Christ as King and His court of worshipping angels about Him. He bought the picture and took it to his own private gallery. There he discovered that the picture had been tampered with; that the orginal figure of the Christ had been cut out and that another figure of Christ, evidently by another artist, had been substituted.

"Then this man of wealth began another search, this time for the missing Christ. He hunted in many lands and, after a great many disappointments, found what seemed to be a reproduction of the picture he already possessed. This also claimed to be a genuine Murillo. He purchased it and took it home. Deftly removing the false Christ from the first picture, he inserted the true Christ from the second picture. And then it was seen that the correct restoration had been made. That picture is hanging to-day in one of the great galleries of Europe, under the title 'The Restored Christ.' " There are many people in our American institutions and churches who have lost Jesus Christ out of their lives because of the apostasy in our education. There is no substitute for Him. Germany tried a substitute but it does not fit. Our great need to-day is for a restored Christ in American education, not merely the "Man of Galilee" but Christ the Son of God, very God of very God—the real, authoritative, saving, miracle-working Christ.

CHAPTER IX

THE REMEDY—ORGANIZATION

WE have no desire to see organizations multiplied, especially organizations of new religious denominations, for is not the world top heavy with them to-day? Some subordinate organizations are vital to the welfare of the Church—our missionary and educational societies, for example —while others serve a temporary purpose only; and when these have done their work they should retire from the field. There are organizations that are greatly needed, and without which the churches could not do their work.

IS A NEW ORGANIZATION NEEDED?

It seems that a new organization (not a new religious denomination) would serve a large purpose at this time in the life of the churches, as an aid to help bring about a solution of the question we are discussing. The task is so great that it is wondered whether the desired results can be obtained without an efficient organization, unless our good God should do something of an extraordinary nature, out of the ordinary way of bringing about helpful reforms. We know that God uses means to accomplish his purposes.

THE VALUE OF ORGANIZATION

A few persons can do with organization what a vast number would find it difficult to accomplish otherwise. This is trebly true if the organization is backed by strong financial support. And even without such support, organization can usually accomplish what men cannot do as well if left disassociated. While it is necessary that the local churches educate their people from the pulpits and otherwise, and also make their protests as churches and individuals to those institutions, as discussed in the previous chapter, nevertheless, the strong and rapidly growing sentiment in America against our modern religious and political perils needs to be crystallized, or organized, and directed to the most effective expression, that is, if this powerful sentiment would do its greatest work.

REASONS FOR ORGANIZATION

Following are a few reasons why some kind of organization would serve a large purpose to-day:

1. Modernism in education and religion, as well as elements of a political danger, have won to their support forces of commanding influence in many parts of America. Some of these elements represent well-known financial, political and religious organizations. It is believed that these powers can best be opposed and their influence and activities defeated by counter-organization.

2. The time will come when protests from churches and individuals made to our educational institutions will not be sufficient. If these protests should be numerous during the next few years they would accomplish far reaching results. But as has been stated, heretofore, our institutions are becoming rich, men and women are bequeathing millions to them, and already some of the universities, both large and small, have immense endowments. It is clear, therefore, that many of our educational institutions will, in the near future, he independent financially; and we know that this will give to these institutions a sense of security and independence of the local church, or of any individual however influential he may be.

But these institutions cannot get along without students. There is only one way to properly, adequately, and accurately represent these institutions to the American people, and that is by an organization that covers every part of America. Activities showing the true character of the work of any educational institution could be directed from the parent society in New York, and carried out by all the local societies throughout the Nation. This local influence at work everywhere, with literature provided, and by personal endeavor, could ultimately and permanently bring to terms the largest educational institutions as well as the smallest.

3. What is true of the educational institution

is also true of the local church. How can a preacher, for example, be silenced in a local church? It can be done by a well directed and wisely conducted campaign against his teachings. With able men and women representing every local evangelical church in this new organization, writing letters to the members of the church, and bringing influence to bear upon the officials of the church and others throughout the community, against the false teacher, in public press, and in pulpit if possible, and through other channels, it would be impossible for the New Theology teacher to long endure such a holy and worthy publicity and propaganda against him. Moreover, his own church would, in all probability, under such continuous pressure, rise up and demand that their minister should seek another field. Once out of the pulpit this splendid organization would see that the false teacher does not get another church in America. Surely such service as this would be an honor to God and untold blessing to His Church and Kingdom.

4. This sort of an organization will be needed more and more because the teachers in many of our institutions who are allied with the advocates of the New Theology are already exerting their influence to prevent, so far as possible, any Old Theology preacher from getting a call to a church. This influence is already felt in some quarters, emanating from certain universities and backed by powerful financial influence, and it will, doubt-

less, increase. The evangelical churches, including their pastors will *soon be compelled* to take vigorous action in behalf of their own protection and welfare, and that of the cause of Jesus Christ generally. Within three months the writer has had proof of this boycott in various parts of America, on the part of Association and State officials, shutting out from pulpits, and even from ordination, every candidate who said that he believed in the Second Coming of Christ.

5. An organization is needed by men and women of like mind because it seems next to impossible for the local churches, or for individuals to-day, to get any of our large Church Societies to protest to the educational institutions, or to undertake any united action against the religious teachings in our institutions. The reason for this is, that these Boards are oft-times divided among themselves, having members who are friendly to Modernism. Our Evangelical Bodies, therefore, *are frequently divided at the top,* and this division would serve to block the way to any powerful united action. Furthermore, the financial powers referred to are influential with these Boards; and human nature, as it is, weak and easily influenced by worldly power, would, in many cases, yield to pressure from that quarter. Because of this, a way should be found to bring great influence upon, or to break through, or to control, or avoid these Boards and strike directly at the source of our problem—the educational institutions. Indeed it is

largely probable that with the noblest men and
women in the local churches strongly organized,
and carrying on such exalted service, the various
boards and societies of the Churches could be
prevailed upon to elect only those to membership
who are opposed to the New Theology.   The
National Conventions or Conferences or Presbyteries or Assemblies, or Governing Bodies could
probably be controlled also, by directing in the
appointment of delegates from the local churches
or from other bodies.   Also by the same
kind of service could influence be exerted in the
election of trustees and boards of our various
educational institutions, and thus the organization
could be helpful everywhere in determining the
type of men who should serve in positions of large
responsibility.

6. A society of the kind indicated could
render valuable aid to the nation in times of
political crises, when delicate matters demand a
settlement—matters of a serious nature, and to
which reference need not be made here.   There
could be no rivalry with other societies of a
patriotic character, but rather at times helpful
cooperation.   All will be needed more and more
as the years roll by.   There is a certain society
to-day, controlled by a powerful organization, the
political intrigues of which may have to be opposed by a still stronger body of American
citizens.   Any autocratic power that works in
secret to thwart helpful reforms is a danger to

the liberties of the American people, and, as such, should be defeated at the ballot box. The time may come when this Nation will be compelled, in behalf of the religious and political liberties of the people, to defeat this religious autocracy. If such an emergency should arise, a powerful society, made up of the best religious elements in the Nation would be of incalculable value.

The chief function of such an organization, however, would not be political, but to protect the interests of Evangelical Religion.

It would be difficult to enumerate the value of such a society. Its literature would be widely distributed. Thousands of our young people, as well as others who are in danger of becoming ensnared by Modernism, would become enlightened and Christianized, and thus the whole nation would be touched and reached for higher and nobler things. There is little doubt that through it every denominational agency and educational institution, that is, in anywise, connected with the churches, could be prevented from pursuing any method in education antagonistic to the Bible as a divine Revelation. It could in all probability succeed in cutting off most of the financial support from these institutions, if not finally bringing about their total destruction; that is, should such method be deemed necessary in behalf of the cause of Jesus Christ.

The reader is advised to discuss this matter with men of sound sense and loyalty to the Truth.

The pastor of the local church who has not been ensnared by the modern heresies, also prominent laymen who are loyal to the Truth would be the proper parties, after prayerful counsel, to initiate the planting of a society in their community.

THE NAME:

The name of such a society could easily be given. It is possible that before this book reaches the reader its name and character may be determined. If further information is desired application may be made to the author.

Unless local conditions prevent, it would be necessary to organize on a union basis. The Society should be made up of members of local churches in good standing. Before proceeding to form an organization it would be necessary to procure literature from headquarters.

The chief purpose of this volume, it should be said, is not to create a new denomination, or even an organization of any sort, but rather to co-operate with God and His people in bringing to pass the much needed reforms in our modern education. If an organization is necessary to this high end, then let the lovers of God and His Word proceed forthwith and effect everywhere such an organization; but if this should be deemed inexpedient, let them act promptly upon the suggestions outlined in this volume. The Word of our God will stand.

The Modern Conflict Over the Bible .

By

G. W. McPHERSON

SECOND EDITION
REVISED and ENLARGED from 164 to 350 PAGES

---

*This volume is handsomely bound, cloth, gold letters,
large readable type.*

The first edition (paper), 25,000 copies, has been read in many parts of the civilized world, and recommended by thousands. Some individuals have taken hundreds of copies for free circulation. The *second edition*, which issues from the press in June, 1919, is a *more valuable*, scholarly and comprehensive discussion of all the great teachings of the Bible, and vital present-day religious problems. *Every page is alive with interest*, and grips the thought, and arouses the noblest impulses to action. A noted authority who read part of the manuscript said: "This book with its companion volume, 'THE CRISIS IN CHURCH AND COLLEGE,' should create a new era in religious education." It contains a few of the most valuable chapters found in "THE CRISIS IN CHURCH AND COLLEGE," and, like the latter, grapples with the problem of religious education. The chapters on: *Modernism And Apostolic Christianity*, and, *The Church And Its Message One*, are worth the cost of the book. No religious student can afford to be without this volume in his library.

Sold by the Author at 34 St. Andrew's Place, Yonkers, N. Y.

Price $1.50; postage additional, 20 cts.

One of the largest publishers in America asked permission to introduce these books. The Author, however, decided to be his own publisher, and thus make sure that these volumes would reach the source of our religious problem—the educational institutions and the clergy.